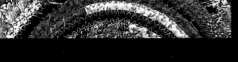

S0-AGH-758

It's a Wrap

SEWING FABRIC PURSES, BASKETS, AND BOWLS

Susan Breier

STACKPOLE BOOKS

Essex, Connecticut

Blue Ridge Summit, Pennsylvania

STACKPOLE BOOKS

An imprint of Globe Pequot, the trade division of
The Rowman & Littlefield Publishing Group, Inc.
4501 Forbes Blvd., Ste. 200
Lanham, MD 20706
www.rowman.com

Distributed by NATIONAL BOOK NETWORK
800-462-6420

Copyright © 2006 by Susan Breier
First Stackpole Books edition 2024

Credits

Technical Editor: Dawn Anderson
Copy Editor: Sheila Chapman Ryan
Illustrator: Laurel Strand
Cover and Text Designer: Stan Green
Photographer: Brent Kane

All rights reserved. No part of this book may be reproduced in
any form or by any electronic or mechanical means, including
information storage and retrieval systems, without written
permission from the publisher, except by a reviewer who may
quote passages in a review.

The contents of this book are for personal use only. Patterns herein
may be reproduced in limited quantities for such use. Any large-
scale commercial reproduction is prohibited without the written
consent of the publisher.

We have made every effort to ensure the accuracy and
completeness of these instructions. We cannot, however, be
responsible for human error, typographical mistakes, or variations
in individual work.

British Library Cataloguing in Publication Information available
Library of Congress Cataloging-in-Publication Data available
ISBN 978-0-8117-7495-6 (paper : alk. paper)
ISBN 978-0-8117-7496-3 (electronic)

Printed in India

DEDICATION

To all the women who have no idea what they want to be when they grow up, even though they are now grown up! To all of the women who are still wondering "What is my purpose in life?" and "What will make me feel fulfilled?"

Be patient; you are learning and growing each day. Be kind to others and be kind to yourself. There is a plan for you as there is for me.

You may have great plans or you may not have a clue what the future might hold. If you want to accomplish something, work toward making your dream a reality. Patience is not only important—it is also a gift.

Make an assessment of your God-given talents. Whatever they may be, allow them to grow. If your talent is sewing or crafts, develop that area of your life. You will be in good company.

Be realistic. Not everyone will be world famous, a gifted brain surgeon, or Mother Teresa. We can only aspire to use our talents to the best of our ability and share those talents with others.

My wish for you is that you enjoy each stage of your life, love your family, set a good example for others, and find your purpose. Along the way, you will help others by your example.

Take care of yourself and everything else will fall into place. Each person is very valuable—including you!

ACKNOWLEDGMENTS

My husband, Jeff, has supported me during this writing experience. We have both grown tremendously through this process. He has encouraged me each day to do my best and has helped me in many ways. Thank you, Jeff.

Our sons and their wives—Chris and Carolyn, Scott and Jenny—have waited patiently for the projects that they would like me to make for them. Thank you for your interest in my passion for sewing and your understanding of my desire to share these projects with others.

Both my mother and father, Lucille and Donald Rothenbach, were there to help me as a child with my many projects. My aunt Marion Pope gave me additional praise for my crafts and made me feel special. All three are deceased but I will never forget the part they played in my life.

A special thank-you to Linda and Michael Reuss Benson from Fabric Fusions in Brown Deer, Wisconsin. They were the first to see my completed projects and immediately encouraged me to write a book. Their praise meant all the difference in how I perceived my projects. They made me think I did have something worthwhile to share!

Many friends, students, and shop owners have shown genuine enthusiasm about my work and the process involved. They too encouraged me to write this book.

A sincere thank-you to Martingale & Company staff for giving a new writer a chance to share her love of sewing.

Preface

Life is changing very fast. High-tech inventions leave me feeling out of touch. World problems frustrate me. There is so much that I don't understand in life.

Hobbies help me stay active, learn new things, and keep up with what is new. The art of sewing and quilting has helpful rules to follow. If I get confused, there are usually written directions to help me. I can do a project at a leisurely pace. I feel great when I create something special using skills that I've learned.

At this stage of my life, I've chosen to be good to myself. If you drop in on me, you will find me at peace in my sewing studio, dreaming up new ideas. I've waited a long while for time for myself. With God's help I will make the most of it.

Contents

Introduction   7

General Materials   8

Basic Techniques   10

Plates   20

Round Baskets   26

Oval Baskets   30

Square Baskets   34

Purses   38

Lids   44

Handles   52

Embellishments   61

Gallery   68

Resources   79

About the Author   80

Introduction

Are you ready for some carefree sewing? This wrapping and coiling technique is very easy and produces great results. Anyone from a beginner to a seasoned sewer will enjoy these projects—and once completed, they won't be stashed at the back of the closet or under the bed! Students in my classes always achieve a nice end result—and they have fun, too.

To COMPLETE THESE PROJECTS, you can use any sewing machine (whether old or new, basic or top-of-the-line) that has settings for straight and zigzag stitches. Making these baskets is a relaxing break from other sewing projects you might have in the works.

The best part about making one of these baskets is the personal reward of designing a one-of-a-kind piece without an exact pattern. Many of you are accustomed to having directions to follow. Now is the time to break free from this format and trust your instincts and use your creative abilities. Yes, I said your creative abilities!

So many basket variations are possible. Page through this book and view just a sampling. You have the option of starting a piece and changing your mind midstream. Sometimes a piece will whisper, "I want a lid," or "Make my brim wider." This is your chance to make the project just the way you want it.

Whether you use a new piece of fabric fresh from a shop or scraps from past projects, you will surprise yourself with how much creativity you have.

General Materials

All the plates, baskets, bowls, and purses in this book are created from clothesline and fabric, using simple wrapping and coiling methods and zigzag stitching. This section provides all the basic information you will need to get started on your project.

Most projects in this book can be made from just a few materials and minimal tools and equipment. For purses, you may need handle or closure hardware in addition to the regular supplies. If you choose to embellish your project, you will want to have a selection of embellishment materials on hand as well. Below is a list of the items most often required.

FABRIC

The best fabric for most projects is 100%-cotton fabric that's been prewashed. Avoid bulky fabrics such as flannel. Multicolored prints look great and hide mistakes better than solid colors. Batiks work wonderfully; because of their higher thread count, they don't fray very much. These projects are ideal for using up leftover scraps (see the baby scrap basket on page 73).

Avoid decorator fabric at first because it's too bulky. It can be used in some projects when you're more experienced with wrapping and coiling. The fabulous designs and textures of decorator fabric work well when making the whole-cloth fabric plate (page 22).

Try for some contrast in your fabric selection because it adds interest to the finished project. Ugly fabrics and prints that you wouldn't normally pick out are fine if the colors are right. The fabric designs change in the sewing process because of the wrapping, and part of the fun is to see a new pattern emerge.

Use the yardages listed at right as a guideline. In most cases, the yardage listed is generous. Depending on the width of the fabric strips used for wrapping and how closely the wraps are made, it should take about a 22" length of fabric to cover about 1' of clothesline. Be sure to purchase enough fabric to allow for any changes you'd like to make to the pattern, such as increasing the height or size or adding a lid.

- 1¾ yards of fabric for a large purse
- 1½ yards of fabric for a medium purse
- 1¼ yards of fabric for a small purse
- 1½ yards of fabric for a large basket or bowl with a lid
- 1¼ yards of fabric for a small or medium basket or bowl with a lid
- 1 yard of fabric for a large basket or bowl
- ¾ yard of fabric for a small or medium basket or bowl
- ¾ yard of fabric for an 11" to 12" plate

BASIC SUPPLIES

The items listed below are frequently used in making the projects shown in this book. Additional embellishment supplies may also be required, depending on the project you choose to make.

Closure hardware. If you are making a purse, use the hardware of your choice or one package of Snag-Free Velcro.

Clothesline. I recommend ³⁄₁₆" poly-reinforced cotton clothesline. You will use about 15 yards for an 11½" plate and 30 yards or less for a small or medium basket. Larger baskets or purses could take 50 yards or more. See "Resources" (page 79) for more information about suitable types of clothesline. Not all types of clothesline are suitable for these projects.

Fabric glue stick (acid free). This type of glue is used for securing the fabric to the clothesline and for holding some embellishments in place until they can be stitched permanently.

Fray Check. Use Fray Check to secure threads after hand stitching embellishments, such as buttons and beads, to a project.

Iron-on adhesive. Use your favorite fusible web or HeatnBond Lite for fusible appliqués. Use HeatnBond UltraHold for creating curled embellishments such as flowers and streamers (see "Dimensional-Fabric Embellishments" on page 63).

Purchased purse handles. A variety of purse handles are available at craft and fabric stores. A handle can also be made by covering 1"-wide nylon or polyester webbing or clothesline with fabric.

Sewing machine oil and cleaning brush. Oil your bobbin case after eight hours of sewing and brush it out regularly; these can be very linty projects!

Tacky glue. Use tacky glue for securing large embellishments or handles in place before hand sewing them permanently in place. Test the glue on scrap fabric first. If it doesn't dry clear, use it sparingly, especially on dark fabrics, where excess glue will easily show.

Tape. Use tape to mark a point on the base of the project where changes will occur. I use green or blue painter's tape or masking tape, all of which can be easily removed.

Thread. Select a thread color that will either match or blend with the fabrics used. I sometimes change colors to match certain areas of the project so that the zigzag stitching is less visible.

Two-step clear epoxy glue. Use this adhesive for attaching embellishments that can't be stitched to the project.

TOOLS AND EQUIPMENT

Appliqué foot or a zigzag foot. An appliqué or zigzag foot allows easy viewing of the area being stitched.

Cutting tools. A rotary cutter, cutting mat, and clear ruler with a printed grid are needed for cutting fabric strips. Scissors will also be necessary.

Hand-sewing needles. A variety of needle sizes is useful. Needles are used for attaching embellishments and handles. Some areas must be sewn by hand because a sewing machine is unable to handle the bulk.

Iron and ironing surface. An iron is used to press bindings or add embellishments with fusible web. There is no need to iron the fabric before rotary cutting your strips (unless it is very wrinkled). Slight wrinkles won't be visible on your wrapped clothesline. A mini-iron works great for fusing appliqués or pressing in small areas.

Machine needles. Use new #80 or #90 universal or Sharp sewing-machine needles. These work well for zigzag stitching rows of clothesline together. Change the needle if your thread breaks often or after every second project.

Measuring tape. This is handy for measuring clothesline and your project's width, length, and height.

Needle-nose pliers. Use these to pull hand-sewing needles through bulky areas of the project when attaching embellishments or handles.

Plexiglas extension table. If you are using an open-arm sewing machine, place a Plexiglas extension table (available at sewing and quilt shops) next to the machine to create a level surface on which to rest the project while stitching. Or, you can create your own extension surface by stacking books next to the arm of the machine until the stack reaches the height of the arm. Be sure the surface is flat and level, because any change in the angle of the project under the needle will change the shape of the project. Although most small projects can be sewn without this aid, it is a must when sewing plates or larger items.

Sewing machine. I use an open-arm machine with a dual-feed feature. A standard machine that has a straight stitch and a zigzag-stitch feature will work well for making most of the projects shown in this book. The ability to drop the feed dogs is also helpful. Dropping the feed dogs allows bulky clothesline to be easily placed under the presser foot. Remember to return the feed dogs to their original position before sewing. Not all machines will produce exactly the same results since each machine is different. Experimentation is the key.

Stiletto or bamboo stick. Either of these tools helps move the project along without getting your fingers too close to the needle. The tools also help hold areas in position when sewing.

Straight pins. These are used to hold glued clothesline or embellishments in place while hand sewing.

Walking foot. A walking foot may be needed depending on how easily the wrapped clothesline moves along under the presser foot.

Basic Techniques

To create the projects in this book, follow the specific directions listed with each project and refer to the basic techniques in this section. Once you understand the basic wrapping, coiling, and stitching techniques and the methods used for shaping a project, it will be easy to create a project using your own design. Keep in mind that medium-sized projects are the easiest to make.

CUTTING FABRIC STRIPS

Colorful strips of fabric are all that is needed to transform ordinary white clothesline into something decorative. It isn't necessary to cut the fabric strips perfectly. It's OK if part of the strip is narrower than another part or if the strips aren't on grain. Because the strips are wrapped around the clothesline, any miscuts will not be apparent. To cut fabric strips from the full width of the fabric, fold the two selvage edges of the fabric together and adjust the fabric so it hangs straight. Fold the fabric again, edge to edge, so you have four layers of fabric. Place the fabric on a cutting mat and position a clear ruler with a printed grid perpendicular to the folded edges. Because I'm not actually measuring the strips, I place the ruler on the fabric side rather than the mat side. This gives me better control. Using a rotary cutter and cutting mat, make a straight cut across the fabric at one edge. Cut the folded fabric into strips that measure ½" to ¾" wide by the width of the fabric. Cut about 10 strips at a time to prevent fraying from handling.

To cut strips from scrap pieces of fabric, cut the strips ½" to ¾" wide and as long as your scrap piece allows. Don't bother with lengths less than 3". It doesn't matter if the pieces are cut on the bias, crosswise grain, or lengthwise grain.

Cutting Strips from a Large Plaid

When using a plaid fabric with varying intensities of color, cut strips with a wavy pattern so that each strip picks up a variety of colors. Cutting straight strips would yield several strips of different colors, which would produce sharp contrasts in the wrapped clothesline and the finished project. Wavy cutting is best for large-scale plaids where the color or value varies greatly.

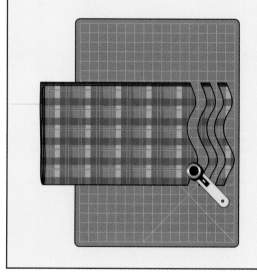

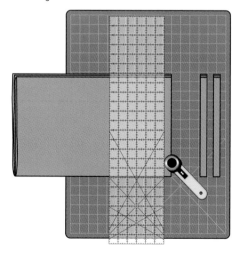

WRAPPING CLOTHESLINE WITH FABRIC STRIPS

1. Make a straight cut at the end of the clothesline to eliminate any frayed ends. Use a glue stick to apply glue to both the end of the clothesline and to the first 1" of the wrong side of the fabric strip. Position the clothesline on the glued portion of the strip as shown, allowing ¼" of the fabric to extend beyond the end of the clothesline. Don't fold the excess fabric allowance over the end of the clothesline. It should remain flat with no clothesline inside. This ¼" area helps to fill the very center of the coil as the project is formed.

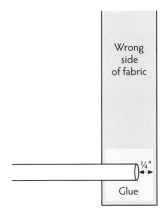

2. Wrap the fabric strip around the clothesline at an angle so that each wrap covers the edge and part of the previous wrap. Use a straight pin to hold the fabric in place at the starting point. Avoid placing the wraps too close together. Always wrap the fabric in the same direction, because changing the direction will show in the finished project. I use the "up, over, and under" wrap, which simply means I wrap the strip from the bottom side of the clothesline and up over the top of the clothesline, and then under the bottom of the clothesline. There is no need to pull tightly; just allow the fabric to firmly encircle the clothesline.

Glue the fabric in place about every 5" or when you feel it's necessary. Overlap the end with another fabric strip, pin, and keep wrapping. Always glue and pin the beginning and ending of each strip in place. When you have about

8" wrapped and the end is glued and pinned, straight stitch down the middle of the clothesline for the first 5" to prevent the fabric from unwrapping at the starting point. If you have difficulty moving the clothesline under the presser foot, refer to "Sewing Guidelines" (page 12). Remove the sewn length from the machine and trim the thread tails.

5"

3. Continue wrapping the clothesline with fabric strips in the same manner until the desired amount of clothesline has been covered. It is best to wrap only a few feet of clothesline at a time. When you need more wrapped clothesline during the construction of a project, simply stop sewing 1" before the end of the wrapping with the needle down. Then, secure additional strips of fabric around the clothesline by gluing, wrapping, and pinning as before. Remove the pins as you come to them.

Creating a Swirling Effect

To produce a swirling effect, choose a striped fabric and cut the strips across the striped pattern. Wrap the strips around the clothesline, always wrapping in the same direction. I use the "up, over, and under" wrap consistently to create a uniform look.

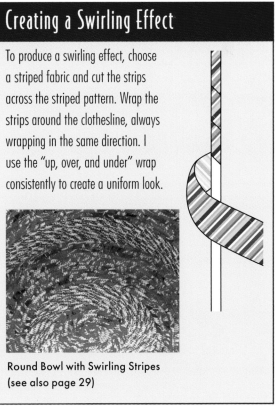

Round Bowl with Swirling Stripes (see also page 29)

JOINING TWO LENGTHS OF CLOTHESLINE

Most projects use one piece of clothesline that's long enough for the whole project. After making a few projects, you will have various lengths of clothesline left over. Don't throw them out—they can be put together very easily to form usable lengths.

To join two lengths of clothesline, first cut about a 16" length of thread in a color that won't show through the fabric strip you plan to use for wrapping. Set the thread aside. Cut the ends of the clothesline that are to be joined so they are straight. Apply fabric glue stick to the end of each piece for 1"; overlap the ends for about ¼" to ½" and hold them together along the glued area. While holding the two pieces of clotheslines together, tightly wrap the 16" length of thread around the joined ends, beginning about ¼" before the overlap and ending about ¼" beyond the overlap. While the glue is still damp, wrap a fabric strip around the join, wrapping that area firmer than normal to make it conform in size to the regular width of the clothesline. Pin the area until it is sewn. It should blend nicely with the remainder of the wrapped clothesline if you give that area a little extra attention.

To join two lengths of clothesline, overlap ends, glue, and wrap with thread. Wrap with a strip of fabric.

SEWING GUIDELINES

The projects in this book are created by stitching rows of fabric-wrapped clothesline together using a zigzag stitch. Each project starts with a coiled base (round, oval, or square) of wrapped clothesline. The project grows as each row is added.

Before starting a project, clean the bobbin case of the sewing machine (follow the instructions in your manual) and install a new #80 or #90 universal or Sharp needle. The needle should be good for a couple of projects, but if your thread starts breaking or you have stitching or tension problems, it may be time to replace the needle again. It makes a big difference in the assembly of the project when you have a clean machine with a new needle.

Attach an appliqué or zigzag foot to your machine and set the machine for a zigzag stitch that is about ¼" wide. Follow the instructions for the project you are making. When you begin stitching, pull on the bobbin and needle threads to help get the clothesline moving through the machine. To join rows of clothesline, simply lay the clothesline next to the piece in the previous row and zigzag stitch, catching about ⅛" of each wrapped clothesline with each stitch. Strive for a uniform zigzag stitch that goes from near the middle of one clothesline to near the middle of the clothesline in the adjoining row. Don't push the rows of clothesline together too tightly. If more thread shows than fabric, adjust the spacing of the zigzag stitch.

An oval base coil is easy to sew. It may be a slower process to stitch the first few rows together at the center of a round base coil. Zigzag stitch one stitch at a time if necessary, stopping with the needle down, raising the presser foot, and turning the base coil slightly before lowering the presser foot and proceeding. After a few stitches, the feed dogs begin to feed the clothesline through the machine. You can also turn the hand wheel to move the presser foot up and down, taking a stitch or two each time, to move the piece through the machine. If bulk is a problem, the feed dogs can be lowered to place the starting piece under the needle. Remember to reengage the feed dogs before starting to sew. If you aren't able to get the wrapped clothesline to move along properly, try using a walking foot.

Zigzag-Stitch and Tension Settings

Before starting your project, make a stitch sample to be sure you have the proper zigzag-stitch setting and the correct tension. Write these settings on a piece of tape and attach it to your machine.

Snip any stray threads from the project as you sew or they may become tangled with the zigzag stitches later and look messy. If the wrapped clothesline becomes tangled around the needle area while you are sewing, simply stop stitching with the needle down and twirl that portion of the clothesline free.

Once the base coil is completed, a piece of tape is adhered to the base to mark the location where all subsequent rows are started and ended, where any changes in fabric or basket shape are made, and where the project is finished off at the end (see "Making Changes" on page 15). Once the base coil is marked with tape, the sides of the basket are formed. Begin sewing where you left off with the base coil, following the directions for your project. Each time you reach the tape mark, a row has been added. Follow the project directions to complete the sides of the basket and finish off at the tape mark, following "Tapering off the Clothesline" (page 18).

You can remove the project from the machine as often as necessary to check the shape. When you're ready to continue, simply insert the project back under the needle and continue where you left off, overlapping the stitching at the new starting point. Each time you change the bobbin, brush out the bobbin case, because these can be very linty projects.

Making a Round Base Coil

1. Create a tight round coil with the wrapped clothesline, starting at the end and coiling until you have a coil about 1¾" in diameter. It may take several tries. If you have difficulty holding the pieces together, you may want to pin or hand baste the rows of the coils in place. Keeping the coil tight (no light should be showing through the center), place it under your presser foot, and straight stitch an X across the coils. This is done to help you zigzag stitch this area without the coil coming apart.

2. Always position the coil under the presser foot so the tail is to the right of the machine needle. Starting at the very center of

the coil, zigzag stitch each coiled row of clothesline to the next coiled row, using a bamboo stick or stiletto to help hold the clothesline in place. Work your way around each row to the end of the starting coil. An ideal zigzag stitch is ¼" wide (see "Sewing Guidelines" on page 12).

3. Continue to wrap, coil, and zigzag stitch additional clothesline around the starting coil until the base coil reaches the size specified in the project instructions. Keep the tail coming through the center area of your machine, to the right of the machine needle, leaving the extra clothesline attached. This is very important! This allows the basket to grow and take shape to the left of the machine where there is ample room. There is not enough room for the basket to be formed to the right of the needle. When your base coil is finished, remove it from your machine, leaving the extra clothesline attached. Use a piece of tape to mark a point near the edge of the base where fabric or shape changes are to take place (see "Making Changes" on page 15).

Making an Oval Base Coil

1. To make an oval base coil, begin with a determined length of wrapped clothesline. This will be the baseline. The remaining wrapped clothesline will be coiled around this length. The baseline measurements are listed for all the oval projects shown in this book. Mark off the baseline length, fold the clothesline in half at that point, and zigzag stitch the two together at the starting fold. An ideal zigzag stitch is ¼" wide (see "Sewing Guidelines" on page 12).

2. Wrap the clothesline around the opposite side of the baseline, turning the corner snugly around the unfilled end of the wrapped clothesline. Zigzag stitch in place using a stiletto or bamboo stick to help hold the clothesline in place. Continue to wrap and zigzag stitch the clothesline around the baseline until the oval base coil reaches the size specified in the project

instructions. Keep the tail coming through the center area of your machine to the right of the machine needle, leaving the extra clothesline attached. This is very important! This allows the basket to grow and take shape to the left of the machine where there is ample room. When your base is finished, remove it from your machine. Use a piece of tape to mark a point near the edge of the base where changes are to take place (see "Making Changes" on page 15).

Front of project

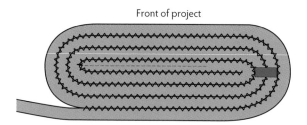

Making a Square Base Coil

1. Follow the directions in "Making a Round Base Coil" (page 13) to make a round base coil of the size specified in the project instructions. Remove the base coil from the machine, leaving the extra clothesline attached.

2. Take your coil to a surface with a grid, such as a cutting mat. Pin the extra wrapped clothesline to the round base, forming a square around the base. Use the lines on the grid as a guide for forming the square.

Front of project

3. Zigzag stitch the four sides of the square to the round base coil at the center of each side. Use a piece of tape to mark the edge along one side of the base where changes are to take place (see "Making Changes" on page 15). Zigzag stitch a second row of clothesline around the square, ending your

sewing at the tape mark. There should be a gap in the base at each of the corners. Fill the gaps in the base with rows of wrapped clothesline cut to fit.

Front of project

4. Zigzag stitch the wrapped clothesline pieces in place at the corners, stitching one row at a time. A stiletto or bamboo stick will help you hold these pieces of clothesline in place while you zigzag stitch them to an adjoining row.

5. Fill any gaps with pieces of wrapped clothesline; glue and then zigzag stitch the clothesline pieces in place. Once you have finished the base, remove it from the machine, leaving the extra clothesline attached.

ADDING A LABEL

When the base coil for a project other than a purse or plate is completed, it's time to add a label to the back. Do it now, because once the project is completed, it may be difficult to fit it under the presser foot to sew on the label. I stitch labels to the inside of purses when the project is nearly complete. I glue labels to the back of plates when completed, following the same procedure as for a basket or bowl (below) but use hand stitching in place of machine stitching. For a basket or bowl, choose a side of the base to be the front of the project and, with the front away from you, flip the base coil over to the other side. Glue the label to the center of the coil so that the tag is parallel to the front of the project. Straight stitch completely around the edges of the label. Remove the base coil from the machine, trim the thread tails, and flip it back over to the right side. The label stitching will be visible on the top side of the project, so use matching thread. Don't cut the wrapped clothesline when you add the label; you will continue wrapping the clothesline around the base to form the sides.

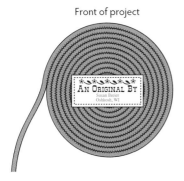

Front of project

Label stitched to the bottom of a round base coil

Making Labels

You can use a purchased label or you can make a label by writing the pertinent information on a small piece of fabric with a Pigma pen. If you're writing your own message, heat-set the ink with an iron before attaching the label to the project.

MAKING CHANGES

Always mark the base coil with a piece of tape at the location where changes are to take place. You may want to draw an arrow on the tape mark using a permanent marker. The tape mark, or arrow, is the point where rows are started and ended, and where your project will change angle positions to achieve the desired shaping. This is also the point where you can change to a contrasting fabric, and where the project will be finished off. As the project grows, and the sides of the basket get taller, it may become difficult to easily see the tape mark. You may want to add a second tape mark, in line with the first one, on the inside edge of the basket so it can be seen as new rows are added. To make any fabric changes and tapering off at the end of a project less noticeable, follow these guidelines:

- If you plan on adding handles to your project, use the side of the project as the point of change. The handles will hide the transitions. I use the right side of the project, so the end of the clothesline will be near the back of the project when the project is finished off.

- If you aren't adding handles, use the back of the project, close to the sides, where changes will be less noticeable.

- If there will be a large embellishment on the front to cover it, make changes at the front of the project.

CHANGING FABRICS

Always use a piece of tape to mark the base coil where changes are to take place. To make a fabric change in a project that isn't a scrappy project, stitch until you come to the tape mark, trim off the remainder of the fabric strip you are working with, glue the end in place, and secure with a pin. Glue and wrap the new strip of fabric around the same piece of clothesline immediately after the previous wrapped fabric and continue stitching. It may be necessary to change the thread on the machine to match the new fabric.

Front of project

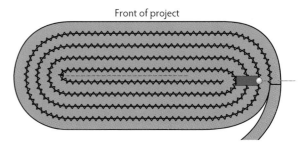

Hiding the Base Fabric

If you are using different fabrics for the base and the side of a project, sew one row of your side fabric as the last row on your base. Doing this prevents the base fabric from peeking through at the sides.

BUILDING UP THE SIDES OF THE PROJECT

To build up the sides of the project, sew additional rows of clothesline to the base coil while holding the base coil in one of four basic angle positions to achieve the desired shaping. The angle position samples (shown on pages 16–18) are stitched with contrasting thread for clarity. Angle positions 1 and 2 are typically sewn for just one row each, to transition from the base to the side of the project. Angle position 3 is used for the sides of the project, and produces a project with sides that angle out slightly. Angle position 3 also has two variations. The first variation produces a project with sharply angled sides and resembles a V shape. The second variation uses a fingertip lift, which produces a project with nearly straight sides. Remember that not all machines will produce exactly the same results because each machine is different. The distance the needle is from the side edge of the machine influences how the basket takes its shape. Built-in cabinet machines might be limited when stitching in angle position 4, which is most often used as an optional step for creating a rolled upper edge on a project. Follow the instructions for your project to determine which of these angles to use and in what order.

Angle Position 1

This angle position creates a gradual transition from the base coil to the sides. Use this angle to begin shaping a curved outer edge on a flat base coil. Place the base coil under the presser foot at the location of the tape marker. Place the fingertips of your left hand, palm up, under the outer half of the base. Don't lift up; the positioning of your fingertips underneath as you sew will produce the correct amount of curve around the outer edge of the piece. Be sure to rest your fingers on the bed of the sewing machine as shown. Stitch one row around the base, holding your hand position the same until you return to the tape mark, and then stop with the needle down. The row just stitched should be raised slightly above the base coil. Begin and end each row at the tape mark.

Angle Position 2

This angle position creates a sharper transition from the base coil to the sides. Use this angle to gradually build the curve in the basket where the clothesline rises up from the base coil. With the base coil under the presser foot, lift the base coil up midway between the bed of the machine and the flat vertical side edge of the machine. Starting at the tape mark, stitch one row around the project, holding your hand position the same until you return to the tape mark, and then stop with the needle down.

Angle Position 3

This angle position creates a basket with slightly angled sides. Use this angle to complete the curve in the basket where the clothesline rises up from the base coil and continue in this position to complete a basket with slightly angled sides. See "Basic Round Basket" on page 27 for an example of this basket shape. With the project under the presser foot, lift the base coil with your left hand until the coil touches the vertical side of the sewing machine. Starting at the tape mark, stitch one row around the project, holding the same hand position and continuing past the tape mark to complete the transition from flat base to side. For a project with slightly angled sides, continue stitching rows around the project in this position until the project reaches the desired height. Stop stitching 2" before you reach the tape mark on the last row and follow the project instructions to finish the project. (Photos shown top right.)

Begin sewing in angle position 3 with the base coil touching the vertical side of the machine.

As the project grows in angle position 3, it should continue to touch the vertical side of the machine as rows are added.

Angle position 3 has two additional variations (see below). Use variation 1 to produce a basket with more angled sides (V-shaped basket), and use variation 2 to produce a basket with less angled sides (straight-sided basket). See page 27 (top photo) for an example of a V-shaped bowl and see page 29 (bottom photo) for an example of a basket with straight sides.

Angle Position 3, Variation 1 (V-shaped basket)

In order to make this basket, your machine bed must be level with the surrounding work surface to prevent distorting the basket. A Plexiglas extension table is ideal.

With the project under the presser foot, lift the base with your left hand until the coil touches the vertical side of the sewing machine as shown in the top left photo on this page. Starting at the tape mark, stitch one row around the project, holding the same hand position and continuing past the tape mark to complete the transition from flat base to side. Continue stitching rows around the base coil in the same manner until you feel the machine bed taking over the shaping of the basket. It sounds strange, but it does happen! If you let the machine bed or the work surface guide the project, you will get a wider opening, and the sides of the basket will angle out sharply. Continue stitching rows of clothesline around the basket, letting the machine bed do the shaping, until the side of the basket reaches the desired height. Stop stitching 2" before you reach the tape mark on the last row and follow the project instructions to finish the project.

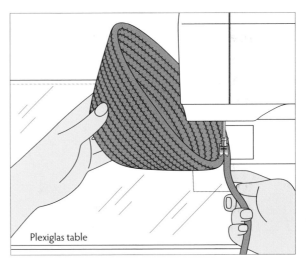

Plexiglas table

V-shaped basket

Angle Position 3, Variation 2 (Straight-Sided Basket)

For projects with high sides, it's best to have the machine bed level with the surrounding work surface to prevent distorting the basket. This variation works particularly well on projects that are large enough to clear the top of the machine as rows are being added.

With the project under the presser foot, lift the base with your left hand until the coil touches the vertical side of the sewing machine as shown in the top left photo on this page. Starting at the tape mark, stitch one row around the project, holding the same hand position and continuing past the transition from flat base to side. Continue stitching rows around the base coil in the same manner and as soon as it becomes possible, wedge the fingertips of your left hand under the project. As the project becomes larger, insert your fingertips further under the side of the project, but only as far as the first knuckle. This slight fingertip lift will produce a basket with a straighter side. For large baskets that encircle the side edge of the sewing machine, keep the base coil parallel to the side edge of the machine as the basket grows. Regularly take the basket out from the machine and examine it to see how the sides are shaping up and make any needed adjustments. Continue stitching rows of clothesline around the basket until the sides of the basket reach the desired height. Stop stitching 2" before you reach the tape mark on the last row and follow the project instructions to finish the project.

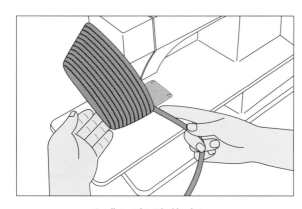

Small straight-sided basket

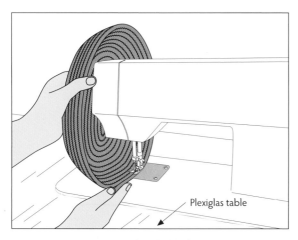

Large straight-sided basket

Angle Position 4 (Rolled Edge)

This angle is used to build a rolled outer edge on a basket after the desired height has been achieved. Remove any extension tables from your machine. Place the project under the presser foot at the tape mark with the edge of the project on the arm of the sewing machine. Push the remainder of the project lower than the machine bed at the side edge. Zigzag stitch around the project for the number of rows indicated in the project instructions (usually three to five), stopping 2" before you reach the tape mark on the last row; follow the project instructions to finish the project. Use your hands to roll the top edge of the basket over.

Create a rolled edge by pushing the project down, lower than the machine bed for the last few rows. This photo shows the project near completion. Usually the edge does not roll over on its own. Use your hands to shape the rollover.

TAPERING OFF THE CLOTHESLINE

Unwrap the clothesline and cut it 1¼" past the tape mark. Do not cut the fabric yet. Starting at the tape mark, gradually trim the clothesline along the length at an angle to reduce the bulk, trimming the most near the very end of the clothesline. Apply glue to the wrong side of the fabric strip (not the clothesline) and then wrap the remaining clothesline very tightly until you are wrapping only fabric. Trim off the excess fabric. Hold the remaining tail very snugly to the project using a stiletto or bamboo stick and zigzag stitch it in place. Continue to zigzag stitch over the last row of clothesline along the outer edge of the project until you reach the end. Remove the project from the machine and trim the thread tails.

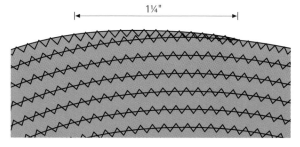

1¼"

Taper the end of the clothesline to blend it into the outer edge of the basket.

Reshaping a Bumpy Ending

If your tapered clothesline doesn't blend in smoothly with the outer edge of the basket and results in a small bump, simply squeeze or finger-press the clothesline at that point while the glue is still wet to compress it and create a smoother transition. Hold the area in place with pins until dry. Do not push the pins in too deeply or that might result in small indentations.

CORRECTING MISTAKES

Often when you make mistakes on these projects, you don't need to get out the seam ripper! Mistakes are usually easy to correct or camouflage. Here are some suggestions for correcting mistakes.

- If your sewing line strays, go back over it a second time the correct way.

- If you notice a spot of exposed clothesline showing, you can dab some color over it using a matching permanent magic marker. Or, if the exposed gap is large, simply take a snip of fabric, glue it over the spot, and zigzag stitch over it.

- If you see light through the center of a base coil, apply glue to a small piece of fabric, wedge it into that area, and stitch in place.

Preventing Floppy Baskets

Long baskets or very large baskets have the potential to become floppy. Use the guidelines below to prevent or correct floppiness.

- Use a slightly tighter zigzag stitch when constructing the basket.
- Choose a fabric with a high thread count.
- Use fabric glue more often when wrapping the clothesline, but remember to use it lightly.
- Wrap the clothesline with a 2" double binding at the top of the basket for more strength.
- Stitch wrapped clothesline in a decorative pattern around the sides of the basket (see French Bread Basket on page 32).
- Use Aleene's Fabric Stiffener on the basket. After adding wrapped clothesline in a decorative pattern to the sides of the French Bread Basket for support, I felt it needed something more. To further stiffen the basket, I used a spray bottle to lightly cover it with a mixture of one-half stiffener and one-half water. I then allowed the basket to air-dry on a wire rack. The solution dried clear, left no residue, and stiffened my basket. It's best to start with a light application first. Another coat can be added later, if needed.

CARE INSTRUCTIONS

When a finished project gets dusty, vacuum it lightly. If it's soiled, spot clean with a little soap and water first. If that doesn't work, hand wash it in cool water with a gentle detergent; rinse thoroughly. Air-dry after reshaping. Please don't try to machine wash these items because it might fray some of the edges of the fabric strips or damage the embellishments.

Avoid placing your fabric projects in the sunlight because they will fade over time. Also, don't use any fabric softener at any time during the process—it will stop fusibles from bonding and make the project floppy.

Plates

Choose from two basic fabric-plate designs: a coiled plate, below, and a whole-cloth fabric plate, shown on page 22. The coiled version showcases the rows of wrapped clothesline, while the whole-cloth fabric plate conceals the coiled clothesline with a top layer of fabric. The whole-cloth plate offers the opportunity to use a fun novelty print and do some decorative machine quilting over the plate. Most of the plates in the book measure 11½" in diameter, but you can make them any desired size.

SCRAPPY RUSSET-COLORED COILED PLATE

COILED PLATE

To get the feel for the wrapping, coiling, and stitching techniques used in this book, start with this coiled plate project, since a coiled plate can be finished in just a few steps. Once you have mastered the techniques it will be easy to move on to the other projects in the book. A coiled plate can be made from a single fabric or a variety of scraps, as shown opposite.

Finished Measurements
Plate diameter: 11½"

Materials

See "Basic Supplies" (page 8) and "Tools and Equipment" (page 9).
15 yards of clothesline
¾ yard or scraps of fabric

How to Make a Coiled Plate

Refer to "Cutting Fabric Strips" (page 10) and "Wrapping Clothesline with Fabric Strips" (page 11) to prepare the wrapped clothesline for this project.

1. Follow steps 1 and 2 for "Making a Round Base Coil" (page 13). It's very important to keep the coil in a flat position as it grows. If you are using an open-arm machine, use an extension table. Continue to wrap, coil, and zigzag stitch rows of clothesline together until the coil reaches a diameter of about 10½", or is two rows away from the finished plate size of 11½".

2. To build up the sides of the plate, start by marking the side of the base coil with a piece of tape to indicate where the next two rows will start and finish. Build up the sides around the plate by stitching two rows around the coil in angle position 1 (page 16), stopping 2" before the tape mark on the last row.

3. Finish the plate referring to "Tapering off the Clothesline" (page 18). Add a label to the back (page 14).

PLATE TIPS

Working with Scraps

When making a scrappy project, be careful not to get two of the same fabrics in the same area on adjoining rows or it will be noticeable in the finished project. Vary the length of the fabric strips—using some short strips and some long strips will provide the right scrappy look. You don't have to change thread during the construction of the project. Remember that you want a scrappy look. Sometimes I use a variegated thread on scrappy projects. You can also try using one color of thread for the bobbin and another for the needle.

Ensuring a Flat Base

If the coiled base does not turn out flat, use an iron with steam and a pressing cloth to help block it to a flat position. If necessary, cut a few zigzag-stitched threads to help the project lie flat.

Making a Flat Plate or Wall Hanging

To make a completely flat plate without an upturned outer edge, simply omit step 2 (left) and stitch all the rows of clothesline in the flat position. This technique can be used to create a large, flat wall hanging (see page 78, top photo).

Displaying Plates

Display your plates or flat wall hangings on a wall by securing them in place with Snag-Free Velcro. Or, showcase plates by displaying them on a picture or plate stand. To display the projects on the wall, whipstitch the loop side of a piece of Snag-Free Velcro to the back of the project and secure the matching hook side of the Velcro to the wall using small nails.

WHOLE-CLOTH
PURPLE-AND-YELLOW
PAISLEY FABRIC PLATE

WHOLE-CLOTH FABRIC PLATE

For a whole-cloth fabric plate, there is no need to wrap the clothesline with fabric strips, because the base is covered with a whole piece of fabric after it is completed. Because the clothesline isn't wrapped, the amount of bulk is reduced, making it possible to use a heavier fabric for this project, such as decorator fabric, if you desire. You may want to use a solid coordinating fabric for the back.

The fabric covering the plate is secured in place by stitching over the surface of the plate. For a quilted look, place a piece of thin batting or muslin on the front side of the plate before layering it with your chosen fabric. If your chosen fabric is light in color, line the front surface of the base with a piece of muslin before layering it with the fabric to prevent the coils from showing through the fabric.

The outer edge of this plate is finished off with double binding. For best results, choose a lightweight fabric for the binding.

Finished Measurements
Plate diameter: 11½"

Materials

See "Basic Supplies" (page 8) and "Tools and Equipment" (page 9).
15 yards of clothesline
½ yard of fabric for plate front and back
½ yard of thin batting or muslin (optional)
⅛ yard of binding fabric

How to Make a Whole-Cloth Fabric Plate

1. Follow steps 1–3 of "How to Make a Coiled Plate" (page 21), except don't wrap the clothesline with fabric strips before coiling it.

2. Measure and cut round fabric pieces to cover the front and back of the plate, allowing several inches of fabric to extend over the edges of the plate. Position the plate on a flat surface with the back side up. Apply a glue stick lightly to the back of the plate. (Glue sticks work best; spray adhesives are absorbed by the clothesline and don't hold the fabric in place.) Use a pin to mark the center of the plate, if necessary, to aid in centering any design on the fabric. Position one piece of fabric over the back of the plate and smooth it with your hands, eliminating any puckers. Don't use a layer of batting or muslin on the back of the plate.

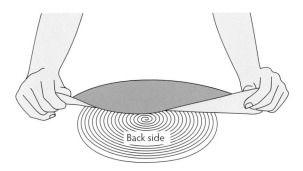

Back side

3. Turn the plate over. Apply a glue stick lightly to the front of the plate. Use a pin to mark the center of the plate, if necessary, to aid in centering any design in the fabric. Layer any muslin or thin batting over the front of the plate, if necessary, and then layer with fabric, applying glue stick as necessary to secure the layers together. Smooth the fabric with your hands, eliminating any puckers. Use straight pins where necessary to hold the fabric in place.

4. Position the plate, layered with fabric, under the presser foot and baste ⅛" from the edge of the plate to hold the layers together. There is no need for the glue to dry before sewing the layers together. Use free-motion quilting to stitch around motifs in the fabric, or stipple quilt as desired (see "Quilting"

on page 25). The more stitching done on the plate, the more the sides of the plate will turn upward.

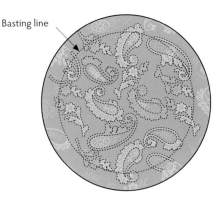

Basting line

Baste the layers together
⅛" from the edge of the plate.

5. Neatly trim the fabric and any muslin or batting layers so you can just see the edge of the clothesline inside. Trim carefully—you only have a slight margin for error. Make sure that your circle is round.

Trim.

6. Bind the edges of the plate (see "Double Binding" on page 67). Add a label to the back (page 14).

SCRAPPY COILED PLATE

Follow the directions for a coiled plate to make this scrappy plate. Take care to use both light and dark fabric strips throughout the plate for a balanced look.

FLORAL PLATE

The layers of this whole-cloth plate were stitched together by following the outline of the flower and leaf patterns. Contrasting binding adds a ribbed appearance to the edge of the plate.

CHRISTMAS PLATE

To create a themed plate with a perfectly coordinated look, use a border print as shown here. Cut a strip from the border to use as the center accent and use the remainder of the yardage for cutting strips to wrap the clothesline. Follow the basic instructions for a coiled plate (page 21). Then use the instructions for a whole-cloth fabric plate (page 22) as a guide for adding the center accent strip, turning under the raw edges of the border strip on the sides. Bind the outer edges of the plate with contrasting binding.

BATIK PLATE

Large stippling was used to secure the layers together on this whole-cloth plate. I used a variegated thread because of the many colors in the fabric. The edge of the plate is bound with matching fabric.

HEART PLATE

Decorator fabric was used for this whole-cloth plate. A layer of muslin was used as a liner on the front side. After following the vertical and horizontal grid in the fabric with straight stitches, the plate almost appears quilted.

Quilting

When making a whole-cloth plate, it's necessary to stitch the fabric layers and the coiled base together. I often use patterned fabrics for these plates and simply use the design lines on the fabric to guide my stitching lines. For easy maneuvering around the design lines, use free-motion quilting. To free-motion quilt, you will need to attach a darning foot and lower the feed dogs on the machine. When doing free-motion quilting, don't turn the fabric under the machine. Instead, place a hand on the fabric on each side of the needle and use your hands to guide the fabric under the needle, so that the needle follows the design in the fabric. To secure layers together when the fabric has no obvious design, try stipple quilting. To stipple quilt, create a pattern of closely spaced curvy lines as shown above.

Round Baskets

Round baskets are very versatile. Making one with just one fabric is fastest, but for more interest you can change colors to produce a striped effect, or add a contrasting binding or embellishments to the finished basket. The instructions for a Basic Round Basket are given opposite. Variations of the basic are shown below and on pages 28 and 29.

URN-STYLE ROUND BASKET

The top and base portions of the urn are each made as individual pieces first and then secured together. For the base of the urn, make a round base coil with a 2¼" diameter. Build up the sides by adding one row in angle position 1, one row in angle position 2, and the remaining rows in angle position 3 until the piece measures ¾" high. For the top of the urn, make a V-shaped basket, starting with a 2¼" round base coil. Stitch in angle position 2 for one row; then use variation 1 of angle position 3 until the basket measures 6" high, and then bind the top edge. Glue the bases of the two pieces together and hand stitch them securely. This basket is accented with a flower embellishment created using HeatnBond UltraHold iron-on adhesive (see "Dimensional-Fabric Embellishments" on page 63). The top of the basket measures 8" across, and the base measures 3¾" in diameter.

BASIC SMALL ROUND BASKET

Define the upper edge of the basket with a contrasting binding and satin cording. Create a focal point by adding a beaded dangle at the center front.

BASIC ROUND BASKET

A round basket is the fastest and easiest to sew. This size is the perfect starter project. It sews up quickly and allows you an opportunity to be creative with embellishments. For ideas, see "Embellishments" on page 61.

Finished Measurements
Height: 3"
Base diameter: 4½"
Diameter across top: 7"

Materials

See "Basic Supplies" (page 8) and "Tools and Equipment" (page 9).
11 yards of clothesline
½ yard of fabric for basket
⅛ yard of fabric for binding (optional)
Satin cording and beads for embellishing (optional)

How to Make a Basic Round Basket

Refer to "Cutting Fabric Strips" (page 10) and "Wrapping Clothesline with Fabric Strips" (page 11) to prepare the wrapped clothesline for this project. Refer to "Basic Techniques" (pages 10–19) for detailed instructions for completing the steps below.

1. Make a round base coil that's 4½" in diameter.

2. Add a label to the back side of the base, if desired.

3. Build up the sides around the base by stitching one row around the coil in angle position 1. Then stitch one row around the coil in angle position 2. Change to angle position 3 and stitch rows around the project until the sides measure 3" high. Stop stitching 2" before you reach the tape mark on the last row.

4. Taper off the clothesline to finish the basket.

5. Apply a 2" double binding to the top edge, if desired (see "Double Binding" on page 67). Add embellishments to the basket, if desired (see "Embellishments" on page 61). This basket has decorative satin cording hand stitched in place just below the bound edge and features a beaded drop at the center front (see "Beads" on page 65).

MEDIUM-SIZED BOWL WITH DIMENSIONAL FLOWERS

Make a round base coil with a 3¾" diameter. Build up the sides by adding one row in angle position 1, one row in angle position 2, and the remaining rows in variation 2 of angle position 3, using the left-hand fingertip lift when possible, until the basket measures 4⅝" high. Apply double binding to the upper edge of the basket. Embellish the basket as shown with dimensional flowers created using HeatnBond UltraHold iron-on adhesive (see "Dimensional-Fabric Embellishments" on page 63). The basket measures 7¼" across the top.

STRAIGHT-SIDED BASKET
WITH A FLARED EDGE

From the collection of Ann and George Kessler.

Make a round base coil with a 6½" diameter. Build up the sides by adding one row in angle position 2. Change to variation 2 of angle position 3, adding the left-hand fingertip lift when possible, and continue adding rows until the basket measures 3" high. Change to angle position 4 and add four or more rows to give the basket a flared upper edge. The basket measures 8½" across the top.

ROUND BOWL WITH SWIRLING STRIPES

Make a round base coil with a 3½" diameter using the main fabric. Change to contrasting fabric. To create contrasting stripes with the swirling effect, refer to "Creating a Swirling Effect" on page 11. Using contrasting fabric, add five rows to the base coil, and then change back to the main fabric and add five more rows. Continuing with the main fabric, build up the sides by adding one row in angle position 1 and one row in angle position 2; then change to angle position 3 and add five more rows. Change to contrasting fabric and continue in angle position 3 for five rows. Change back to the main fabric for seven rows. The basket should be about 4¼" tall and about 11⅛" in diameter across the top.

FLARED-EDGE BASKET WITH FLORAL APPLIQUÉ

Make a round base coil with a 4" diameter. Build up the sides by adding one row in angle position 2; then change to angle position 3 and continue until the basket is 2¾" high. Change to angle position 4 for four more rows to give the basket a flared upper edge. The finished basket measures 3¾" high and 8½" across the top. The front is embellished with a pieced-flower appliqué (see "Appliqué" on page 62).

SHORT, STRAIGHT-SIDED BASKET WITH A CONTRASTING EDGE

Make a round base coil with a 7½" diameter. Build up the sides by stitching one row in angle position 2. Change to variation 2 of angle position 3, adding the left-hand fingertip lift when possible, and continue adding rows until the basket measures 2¼" high. Change to contrasting fabric for three more rows. The finished basket measures about 3" high. Hand stitch a ⅛"-diameter black cord to the top edge of the basket and tie it in the front, accenting the ends with large beads. Sew small black beads along the top of the cord at the top edge of the basket, spacing them about ¼" apart. The basket measures 9" across the top.

Oval Baskets

Oval baskets are as easy to make as round baskets. The main difference is at the starting point. For a round basket, you coil the wrapped clothesline around itself in a circular manner; for an oval basket, you coil the wrapped clothesline around a predetermined straight length of wrapped clothesline (referred to as the baseline). To make a small basket, start with a baseline that measures about 3". To make a medium-sized basket, start with a baseline of about 4½". Either of these sizes would be good for a first project. The instructions for a basic oval basket are given opposite. Variations of the basic form are shown below and on pages 32–33.

MEDIUM-SIZED OVAL BATIK BASKET

From the collection of Linda and Michael Reuss Benson.

This is the basket that inspired this book! Linda and Michael Reuss Benson purchased this basket after I stopped into their shop in Brown Deer, Wisconsin, with my newly sewn collection. Their encouragement was just what I needed. To construct the basket, make an 8" x 5" oval base, starting with a 4" baseline. Build up the sides by stitching all rows in variation 2 of angle position 3. Finish off the basket when it reaches 3¼" high. Add a double binding to the top edge and decorative handles to the sides (see "Basket Handles" on page 53). The top opening measures 10¼" x 6¾".

BASIC OVAL BASKET

This medium-sized oval basket is perfect for holding small loose items that seem to collect around the house. It's a great size to give as a gift, also. This basket is the perfect size to start with if this is your first oval basket. A contrasting stripe was added to the middle of this basket. If you prefer, stitch all the rows using the same fabric.

Finished Measurements
Height: 3¾"
Base dimensions: 6" x 2¼"
Size of top opening: 9¾" x 5¾"

Materials

See "Basic Supplies" (page 8) and "Tools and Equipment" (page 9).
14 yards of clothesline
½ yard of main fabric
⅛ yard of contrasting fabric

How to Make a Basic Oval Basket

Refer to the instructions for "Cutting Fabric Strips" (page 10) and "Wrapping Clothesline with Fabric Strips" (page 11) to prepare the wrapped clothesline for this project. Refer to "Basic Techniques" (pages 10–19) for detailed instructions for completing the steps below.

1. Make a 6" x 2¼" oval base coil, starting with a baseline measurement of 4¾".

2. Add a label to the back side of the base, if desired.

3. Build up the sides around the base by stitching one row in angle position 1 and one row in angle position 2. Change to angle position 3, stitch five rows around the project, and then change fabrics (see "Changing Fabrics" on page 15).

4. Continuing in angle position 3, stitch three rows around the project using clothesline wrapped with a contrasting fabric, and then change back to the original fabric. Continue in angle position 3, stitching seven rows around the project. Stop stitching 2" before you reach the tape mark on the last row.

5. Taper off the clothesline to finish the basket.

MEDIUM-SIZED OVAL STRIPED BASKET
Use oval baskets to hold jewelry, loose change, office supplies, or whatever else needs to be contained.

FRENCH BREAD BASKET

Make a 12" x 3¾" oval base coil, starting with a baseline measurement of 9½". Build up the sides by adding one row in angle position 1 and one row in angle position 2. Change to angle position 3 and stitch until the basket is 3" high. Long baskets have a tendency to become floppy. If the basket is floppy, strengthen the basket following the tips in "Preventing Floppy Baskets" (page 19). The basket shown was strengthened by stitching wrapped clothesline in a decorative pattern around the sides of the basket (see "Wrapped-Clothesline Embellishments" on page 66) and by using Aleene's Fabric Stiffener. Embellish the basket, if desired, with buttons and beads. The top opening measures 14½" x 6".

BANDED PARROT BASKET

For this novelty basket, make an oval base 6¼" x 2¼", starting with a baseline of 5". Build up the sides of the basket by adding one row in angle position 1, one row in angle position 2, and the remaining rows in angle position 3 until the basket is 3¾" high. Stitch a contrasting band of striped fabric around the basket for interest and add a 2" double binding to the top edge. The two parrots used for handles were recycled from a necklace I found on a shopping excursion. What a find! The top opening of this basket measures 10¼" x 5½".

STRIPED BASKET WITH HEART APPLIQUÉ

The instructions for this basket are identical to the Striped Zebra Basket (below), but changing the fabric and the appliqué motif gives the basket an entirely different look. This basket features knotted-loop side handles made from wrapped clothesline (see "Wrapped Clothesline Handles" on page 53).

STRIPED ZEBRA BASKET

Make a 6¼" x 3¾" oval base, starting with a baseline of 3½". Add one row in angle position 2. Change to variation 2 of angle position 3 and stitch five rows, adding the left-hand fingertip lift when possible. Change to contrasting fabric for five rows, and then back to the original fabric for five more rows. The basket should measure 3½" high. The top opening measures 9" x 6". The zebra was fussy cut and fused to a printed fabric, which was then fused to a larger square of black fabric (see "Appliqué" on page 62). Zigzag stitching was used around the edges of the zebra and the printed fabric. The entire piece was secured to the center of the basket with blanket stitches. The heart-style handles were made from wrapped clothesline (see "Wrapped Clothesline Handles" on page 53).

Square Baskets

The square basket is a simple variation of the round basket. After much experimenting with four-sided baskets, I ended up designing my square base by making a round coiled base first, and then creating a square outline around it. I then use additional wrapped clothesline to fill in the gaps in the corners between the square outline and the round base coil. Once the square base is complete, you simply build up the sides until the basket reaches the desired height. Instructions for a basic square basket are given opposite. Variations of the basic form are shown on pages 35–37.

SQUARE BASKET WITH YO-YO FLOWERS

This small square basket features a contrasting base and binding. The front is decorated with yo-yo flowers and Ultrasuede leaves. Assorted beads and buttons accent the flower centers.

BASIC SQUARE BASKET

This basket was made with a contrasting base and double binding to add interest. If you prefer, you can make the whole basket from the same fabric. Optional fabric yo-yos decorate the front. See "Embellishments" (page 61) for additional ideas. If you are designing your own square basket, a good size for the starting round base would be between 3" and 6" in diameter.

Finished Measurements
Height: 3½"
Square base: 5½"
Round base: 4¼"
Diameter across top: 7¾"

Materials

See "Basic Supplies" (page 8) and "Tools and Equipment" (page 9).
15 yards of clothesline
½ yard of main fabric
½ yard of contrasting fabric
Scraps of fabric and Ultrasuede for embellishments (optional)
Assorted beads and buttons for embellishments (optional)

How to Make a Basic Square Basket

Refer to the instructions for "Cutting Fabric Strips" (page 10) and "Wrapping Clothesline with Fabric Strips" (page 11) to prepare the wrapped clothesline for this project. Refer to "Basic Techniques" (pages 10–19) for detailed instructions for completing the steps below.

1. Using clothesline wrapped with the contrasting fabric, make a 5½" square base by first starting with a 4¼" round base coil.

2. Add a label to the underside of the base, if desired.

3. Starting at the tape mark, wrap the clothesline with the main fabric (see "Changing Fabrics" on page 15). With the base in a flat position, zigzag stitch a row of clothesline wrapped with the main fabric around the square. Adding this row of clothesline that's wrapped with the main fabric to the base ensures that the base color won't show at the lower edges of the sides.

4. Build up the sides of the base by stitching one row around the base in angle position 2. Change to angle position 3 and stitch rows around the base until the basket reaches 3½" high. Stop stitching 2" before you reach the tape mark on the last row.

5. Taper off the clothesline to finish the basket.

6. Add a 2" double binding to the basket, if desired (see "Double Binding" on page 67). Add yo-yo flowers to the basket, if desired (see "Yo-Yo Flowers" on page 66). Cut leaf shapes from Ultrasuede and stitch to the basket.

MORE SQUARE-BASKET IDEAS

BASKET WITH A ROLLED UPPER EDGE

Make a 6½" square base by starting with a 5⅜" round base coil. Build up the sides by stitching one row in angle position 2; then change to angle position 3 until the basket reaches 2¾" high. Create a curved outer edge on the basket by changing to angle position 4 and adding three or four more rows. If necessary, bend the top edge of the basket over and finger-press. I wrapped a beaded necklace around the top of this basket for embellishment and tacked it in place. For more embellishment ideas, see "Embellishments" (page 61). The basket measures 9" square at the top, including the rolled edge.

STRIPED BASKET WITH TWISTED SIDE HANDLES

Create this basket by making a 5½" square base, starting with a 4" round base coil. If making the bottom of the basket from contrasting fabric as shown, be sure to use the side fabric for the last row of the square base. Build the sides by adding one row in angle position 2 and five more rows in angle position 3. Change fabrics and stitch 10 rows in angle position 3 to create the stripe, then return to the original side fabric and continue until the basket is 5" high. Make twisted side handles from wrapped lengths of thick clothesline and accent them at the top and bottom with buttons and beads (see "Wrapped Clothesline Handles" on page 53). The basket measures 8½" square at the top.

BASKET WITH CONTRASTING BINDING AND FRAYED HANDLES

To create this basket, make a 6¾" square base by starting with a 5¾" round base coil. Build up the sides by adding one row in angle position 2 and the remaining rows in angle position 3 until the basket reaches 3" high. Add a 2" double binding to the top edge and handles to the sides (see "Wrapped Clothesline Handles" on page 53). The top of the basket measures 8½" square without handles.

STRIPED BASKET WITH LOOPED SIDE HANDLES

Make a 5½" square base by starting with a 4" round base coil. If making the bottom of the basket from contrasting fabric as shown, be sure to use the side fabric for the last row of the square base. Build the sides by starting with fabric 1 (the side fabric closest to the base) and adding one row in angle position 2. Stitch two more rows in angle position 3. Continue to stitch in position number 3 for the remainder of the basket. Stitch three rows with fabric 2, five rows with fabric 3, three rows with fabric 4, and four rows with fabric 5. Apply a double binding to the top edge. The basket should be about 4⅝" high and about 8½" square at the top. The handles were made by covering strips of nylon webbing with fabric (see "Flat Webbing Handles" on page 57).

LOW BASKET WITH BUTTON ACCENTS

Make a 7¼" square base by starting with a 6¼" round base coil. Build the sides by adding one row in angle position 2 and the remaining rows in angle position 3 until the basket measures 2¾" high. Embellish the front of the basket with a row of buttons stitched near the top edge. The basket measures 8¾" square at the top.

SMALL BOWL WITH FLOWER APPLIQUÉ

Create a 4" square base by starting with a 2½" round base coil. Build up the sides by adding one row in angle position 2 and the remaining rows in angle position 3 until the basket is 2½" high. Embellish the front with a fabric flower and center bead. The top of the basket measures 6" square.

Purses

It occurred to me during my basket making that the wrapping and coiling method used for making baskets would be suitable for making purses as well. A purse is basically a narrow oval basket. Sewing your own purse allows you to make the size that is most suitable for your needs, and allows you the opportunity to customize the fabric choice as well as the number and size of the pockets. You can add as many or as few embellishments as you want. Instructions for a basic purse are given on pages 39–41. Variations of the basic style are shown on pages 41–43.

MEDIUM-SIZED PURSE WITH A VELCRO CLOSURE AND PURCHASED HANDLES

BASIC PURSE

The basic purse shape is created in the same way as an oval basket (page 30). You will add handles, closures, and pockets to the purse, however. Following are the basic steps for constructing a purse with purchased handles, pockets, and a Velcro closure. For this purse, I used a lightweight textured fabric and had great results. Even though the purse is narrow, it will open very wide.

Finished Measurements
Height without handles: 7½"
Height with handles 12"
Width across top: 16½"

Materials

See "Basic Supplies" (page 8) and "Tools and Equipment" (page 9).
40 yards of clothesline
1⅞ yards of fabric
⅛ yard fusible web
Purse handles
Snag-Free Velcro
Embellishments, such as decorative thread and beads (optional)

How to Make a Basic Purse

Refer to the instructions for "Cutting Fabric Strips" (page 10) and "Wrapping Clothesline with Fabric Strips" (page 11) to prepare the wrapped clothesline for this project. Refer to "Basic Techniques" (pages 10–19) for detailed instructions for completing the steps below.

1. Make a 10½" x 2" oval base coil, starting with a baseline measurement of 8¾".

2. Build up the sides by stitching one row around the base coil in angle position 2. Change to angle position 3 and stitch coils around the base until the purse reaches 7½" high.

3. Taper off the clothesline to finish the purse.

4. Make and attach pockets to the interior of the purse, if desired (see "Pockets" at right). Then hand or machine stitch a name tag or label to the inside of the purse.

5. Apply a 2" double binding to the top edge of the purse, if desired (see "Double Binding" on page 67).

6. Add purchased handles and a flap with a Velcro closure to the purse as desired (see "Adding Purchased Handles" on page 40 and "Flaps with Velcro Closures" on page 41). Embellish the flap with a rolled strip of fabric that has been secured with a glue stick and wrapped with decorative thread. Hang a beaded tassel from the handle, if desired (see "Embellishments" on page 61 for more ideas).

Making Pockets

- Pockets must be cut on the straight of grain.

- Keep pockets away from the top purse edge so handles, binding, and embellishments can be attached easily—1" down from the top edge is ideal.

- When you stitch your pockets to the inside of the purse, don't stitch them down tight, but rather let them buckle slightly, allowing room for them to be easily opened.

POCKETS

Pockets are much stronger if they are constructed separately from the purse with both a front and back side. I like to do things the easy way, so I make the pocket front and back from one piece of fabric. You can make a single pocket or you can stitch dividing lines in a large pocket to make compartments for several items. You will need to determine the finished size of your pocket, based on the finished size of your purse and your personal preferences. I like to attach a large pocket to both the inside front and back of the purse and stitch a dividing line down the center of each to make four compartments.

1. Determine the desired size of the finished pocket, keeping in mind that the pocket should be placed 1" from the top edge of the purse. Double the determined pocket length to allow for the pocket backing; then add 2" to the determined pocket length for hems on the pocket front and back and 1" to the determined width for two ½" seam allowances. Cut the pocket from fabric.

2. Press under ½" twice along the width of the fabric. Stitch ⅛" from each fold line.

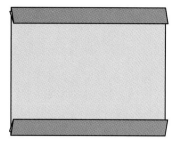

Press under double-fold hems.

Stitch in place.

3. Fold the fabric in half, right sides together, aligning the edges and with the hemmed edges at the top. Stitch ½" seams along the sides. Trim any bulk from the seam allowances and corners.

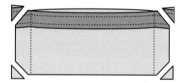

4. Turn right side out and press. If desired, stitch dividing lines in the pocket to create compartments of various sizes.

5. Pin the pocket to the inside of the purse, 1" from the top edge, and stitch to the purse along the side and bottom edges. Stitch the back layer of the pocket to the purse along the top edge of the pocket. The pocket will help protect the zigzag stitches from wear.

ADDING PURCHASED HANDLES

Purse handles are available in many sizes and shapes from craft, sewing, or quilting stores. A sampling of styles can be found on pages 42 and 43. The following steps explain one method for attaching handles to your purse. Other methods are described on pages 41–43.

1. Cut four pieces of 8"-long clothesline, wrap them with fabric, and zigzag stitch along the length of each piece to secure.

2. Align a handle at the center of the purse along the upper edges. Use pins to mark the handle placement on both sides, on both the purse front and back. Be certain to measure and mark carefully so that the handles will fit together evenly when the bag is closed.

3. Securely hand stitch one end of each piece of clothesline to the inside of the purse for 1" at each of the four pin marks. Position a handle on one side of the purse and insert a strip of clothesline through each hole at the base of the handle. Tie two knots in each piece of clothesline. Pin the clothesline pieces in place on the outside of the purse, trimming off any excess. Hold the purse up to check that the handle lines up correctly; make any necessary adjustments. Hand stitch the clothesline pieces in place on the outside of the purse. Repeat for the other purse handle.

FLAPS WITH VELCRO CLOSURES

Velcro closures are a wonderful choice for a purse; just be sure to purchase Snag-Free Velcro. It's available in several colors, so match it to your fabric as closely as possible.

1. Cut two 3½" x 4½" rectangles from fabric and two 3" x 4" rectangles from lightweight fusible web. Fuse a rectangle of web to the wrong side of each fabric rectangle, allowing ¼" around the edges of the web and following the manufacturer's directions. Remove the paper backing.

2. Place the rectangles right sides together and stitch ¼" from the raw edges on one short edge and the two long edges. Trim the corners and turn right side out, pushing out the corners. Topstitch ¼" from the three stitched edges of the rectangle and baste across the remaining (back) edge. Press with an iron to fuse the layers together.

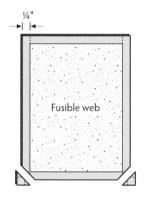

3. Turn under the raw edge on the back side of the rectangle. Pin this edge to the back of the purse, centered across the top purse opening, along the lower edge of the binding. Bring the purse handles together and check that the flap is in the correct position. Then machine stitch the flap in place on the outside of the purse through all layers, taking care not to catch the inside pocket in the stitching. Stitch again over the previous stitching for a secure hold.

4. Cut Velcro to size and position the hook side of the Velcro on the underside of the flap and stitch in place. Close the flap and mark the position of the loop side of the Velcro on the purse front. Stitch the loop side of the Velcro in place. Use the photo below as a guide. If desired, stitch two strips of Velcro on the flap, butted together. This allows the bag to be secured loosely or tightly, depending on how full the bag is.

MORE PURSE IDEAS

SCRAPPY SHOULDER BAG

Make a 7¼" x 1¾" oval base coil, starting with a 5¾" baseline. Build up the sides of the base by stitching one row in angle position 2 and the remaining rows in angle position 3 until the basket reaches 6½" high. To make the shoulder straps, cut two 28" lengths of 1"-wide nylon or polyester webbing and sew a strip of ½"-wide decorative trim down the center of each. Attach the straps to the purse and conceal each of the ends with a button. Use the same method to create the center closure strap for this purse. Attach Velcro under the front end of the closure strap. The bag measures 14¼" across the top.

SMALL PURSE WITH PURCHASED HANDLES AND A BUTTON CLOSURE

To begin this purse, make a 7" x 1¼" oval base coil, starting with a 6" baseline. Build up the sides of the base by stitching one row in angle position 2 and the remaining rows in angle position 3, until the purse reaches 6¼" high. The straps that surround the purse are used to hold the purse handles in place. To make each strap, follow the instructions for "Flat Clothesline Handles" on page 56 using two lengths of bare clothesline. Attach the straps to the purse by hand, adding tacky glue for extra hold. Feed the handles onto the straps at the top edge and hand stitch the ends of the straps to the inside of the purse. The closure is created by stitching two elastic hair bands to the center back of the purse and a large shank button to the front. Secure the elastic bands in place by sewing a ½"-wide piece of fabric over them and turning in all raw edges. The finished purse measures 11" high, including the handles, and measures 14½" wide across the top.

LARGE SCRAPPY TOTE

Make an 11½" x 1¾" oval base coil, starting with a 10½" baseline. Build up the sides of the base by stitching one row in angle position 1, one row in angle position 2, and the remaining rows in angle position 3 until the basket reaches 10" high. For the shoulder straps, overlap and stitch together the ends of a 95½" length of 1"-wide nylon webbing. Cover the webbing with a strip of pieced fabric for a scrappy look (see "Flat Webbing Handles" on page 57), and then edgestitch. Center and attach the covered webbing around the tote as shown. The finished tote measures 20" across the top.

STRIPED PURSE

Make a 9½" x 3¾" oval base coil, starting with a 7" baseline. Stitch five evenly spaced lines across the oval base to help keep it flat and add stability. Build up the sides of the base by stitching one row in angle position 1, one row in angle position 2, and the remaining rows in variation 2 of angle position 3 using the left fingertip lift when possible until the sides reach 2¼"; then change to contrasting fabric and proceed with variation 2 of angle position 3, adding the left-hand fingertip lift for three rows. Change back to the original fabric for 2¼", continuing with variation 2 of angle position 3. Then change to contrasting fabric for three rows. Change back to the original fabric and continue until the purse reaches 8" high. Add pockets and bind the top edge with double binding. Make a strap for each end of each handle by stitching two lengths of bare clothesline together, wrapping the doubled clothesline lengthwise with a fabric strip, and topstitching down the center and side edges. Insert a strap through the hole at the end of the purchased handle, trim the strap to size, and attach the ends of the strap to the purse. Repeat at the ends of each handle.

MEDIUM-SIZED PURSE WITH PURCHASED HANDLES

Make a 7½" x 3" oval base coil, starting with a 6" baseline. Stitch five rows evenly spaced across the finished base for added stability. Build up the sides of the base by stitching in variation 2 of angle position 3, using the left-hand fingertip lift when it becomes possible (after about 2" of sewing). Continue in this position until the purse is 6½" high. Change to contrasting fabric and continue for 1½". Add a double binding to the top edge. To attach each of the purchased handles, two strips of fabric are cut to fit the handle, stitched right sides together along the side edges, and turned right side out. Then the strips are wrapped around the handles, the raw edges are turned under, and the strips are hand stitched to the purse. A yarn embellishment was tied to the handle and a large bead was added as a focal point. The purse measures 8" high and 11½" across the top.

Lids

Lids are easy to sew and draw a lot of attention to your basket. Constructing a lid is similar to making the basket itself. Think of lids as miniature baskets, keeping in mind that the lid grows from the top down. The same angle positions are used for lid construction, but the base coil is much smaller than for a basket. One of the main differences between a basket and a lid is that you leave a hole (or usually two for oval lids) at the start of the base to allow space to insert a handle.

A round basket lid with a contrasting accent stripe and looped handle is shown with its companion basket. Directions for construction of the lid and basket appear on the following pages.

MAKING LIDS

Specific instructions for a round, oval, and square lid are provided in this section, along with their matching baskets. You will need to adjust the lid measurements based on the size of the basket you have made. When constructing your lid, remove it from the sewing machine often to try it on your basket to make sure it fits. You may need to sew more or fewer rows in a position than indicated in the basic instructions for the lid to fit your specific basket. General instructions are also provided for a variety of other lids. Use them and the tips (right) to guide you in creating a lid for your basket.

ROUND BASKET WITH LOOPED-HANDLE LID

The little lid, shown on the facing page, has gotten the most attention out of all the lids I've made. It's easy to construct, and the bright colors give it a lot of punch!

Refer to the instructions for "Cutting Fabric Strips" (page 10) and "Wrapping Clothesline with Fabric Strips" (page 11) to prepare the wrapped clothesline for the project. Refer to "Basic Techniques" (pages 10–19) and "How to Make a Basic Round Basket" (page 27) for detailed instructions for completing the steps that follow.

> **Finished Lid Measurements**
> Height without handle: 2¾"
> Diameter: 7¾"

Materials (for Both the Basket and Lid)

See "Basic Supplies" (page 8) and "Tools and Equipment" (page 9).
15 yards of clothesline
½ yard of main fabric
⅜ yard of contrasting fabric

Constructing Successful Lids

- Always sew the basket first, and then make the lid to fit it.
- Make the lid a complementary shape and size so that it looks as though it belongs with the basket.
- Plan your handle design first (see "Lid Handles" on page 58) so you know how many wrapped clothesline strips will be inserted through the hole at the top of the lid; then you will know how large to make the hole at the top. A ¼" to ½" opening is usually enough because you want the handle to fit snugly in the hole. If the hole becomes too large, remedy the problem by adding embellishments around the handle.
- Stitch a small bead at the front center rim of the basket and on the underside of the lid front. This marks the front of both for a quick matchup.

How to Make the Round Basket

To make the basket for the lid shown opposite, make a round base coil that's 3¼" in diameter using the contrasting fabric. Add three more rows to the base coil using the main fabric. The finished base measures 4½" in diameter. Build up the sides around the base by stitching one row in angle position 2. Change to angle position 3 and stitch four rows with the main fabric. Then stitch three rows with the contrasting fabric, and then five more rows with the main fabric. Taper off the clothesline. Note that the contrasting band is

positioned a little lower than the center of the basket to allow for the lid overhang, which covers the top of the basket. The finished basket measures about 2½" high and has a 6½" diameter across the top.

How to Make the Matching Lid

1. Make a round coiled base of three rows of wrapped clothesline, leaving a ¼" to ½" opening at the starting point to allow for the handle ends to be pulled to the inside later.

2. Build the sides around the base by stitching one row around the base coil in angle position 1, and then stitch one row while in angle position 2. Change to angle position 3 until the lid measures 2½" high. Change to a contrasting fabric (see "Changing Fabrics" on page 15) and stitch three more rows in angle position 3. Change back to the main fabric. Switch to angle position 4 and stitch five more rows around the lid. Check the lid against your basket to be sure it fits and make any adjustments to the size as necessary.

Shaping the Lid

When you use angle position 4 near the edge of a lid, the lid will hug the basket and not slide off as easily.

3. Taper off the clothesline to finish the lid.

4. Add a handle to the lid (see "Looped Handles" on page 60).

OVAL BASKET WITH LID

The lid shown below starts out with a larger base coil than many lids, giving it a flatter surface at the top. The outer edge of the lid is covered in matching binding for a more polished look.

Refer to the instructions for "Cutting Fabric Strips" (page 10) and "Wrapping Clothesline with Fabric Strips" (page 11) to prepare the wrapped clothesline for the project. Refer to "Basic Techniques" (pages 10–19) and "How to Make a Basic Oval Basket" (page 31) for detailed instructions for completing the steps that follow.

Finished Lid Measurements
Height of lid without handle: 2½"
Outer dimensions: 8½" x 6¼"

A small oval batik lid with a flat handle complements the matching oval basket

Materials (for Both the Basket and Lid)

See "Basic Supplies" (page 8) and "Tools and Equipment" (page 9).

13 yards of clothesline

⅝ yard of fabric

How to Make the Oval Basket

To make the basket for the oval lid shown on page 46, make an oval base coil that's 4¼" x 1¾", starting with a baseline of 3". Build up the sides around the base by adding one row in angle position 2 and the remaining rows in angle position 3 until the basket measures 2½" high. Taper off the clothesline. The finished basket measures 7¼" x 5⅛" across the top.

How to Make the Matching Lid

1. Make an oval base coil that measures 4¼" x 1¾", starting with a baseline of 3" and leaving an opening in the coil at each end of the baseline that's just large enough for inserting the handle ends.

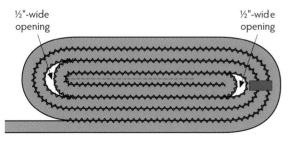

½"-wide opening

½"-wide opening

2. Build the sides of the lid by stitching one row around the base coil in angle position 2. Change to angle position 3 and stitch until the lid is 2½" high. Check the lid against your basket to be sure it fits and make any adjustments to the size as necessary.

3. Taper off the clothesline to finish the lid.

4. Apply a 2" double binding to the outer edge of the lid, if desired (see "Double Binding" on page 67).

5. Make and attach a handle to the lid (see "Flat Lid Handles" on page 58).

SQUARE BASKET WITH LID

A square lid starts out round, and as the lid nears the size of the basket bottom, it's shaped into a square. This gives the lid a flatter surface area at the bottom. The lid for this basket has a multicolored blue, green, and white fabric used as an accent stripe. The contrasting fabric was also used for the base of the basket for a coordinated look.

Refer to the instructions for "Cutting Fabric Strips" (page 10) and "Wrapping Clothesline with Fabric Strips" (page 11) to prepare the wrapped clothesline for the project. Refer to "Basic Techniques" (pages 10–19) and "How to Make a Basic Square Basket" (page 35) for detailed instructions for completing the following steps.

A medium-sized square lid, with ring-style handle, tops off a simple square basket.

Finished Lid Measurements

Height without handle: 5"

Outer dimensions: 8½" x 8½"

Materials (for Both the Basket and Lid)

See "Basic Supplies" (page 8) and "Tools and Equipment" (page 9).
30 yards of clothesline
⅞ yard of main fabric
⅜ yard of contrasting fabric

How to Make the Square Basket

To make the basket for the square lid shown opposite, make a 6" x 6" square base coil, starting with a 4½" round base coil using the contrasting fabric. Change to the main fabric for the side of the basket and add one more row to the base coil. Build up the sides around the base by adding one row in angle position 2 and the remaining rows in angle position 3 until the basket is 3" high. Taper off the clothesline. The finished basket measures 7¾" square across the top.

How to Make the Matching Lid

1. Make a round coiled base of three rows of wrapped clothesline, leaving a ½" opening at the starting point to allow for the handle ends to be pulled to the inside later (see illustration on page 46, step 1).

2. Build the sides of the lid by stitching one row around the base coil in angle position 1, and then stitch one row around the base coil in angle position 2. Change to variation 1 of angle position 3 and stitch until the lid measures 2" high. Change to a contrasting fabric (see "Changing Fabrics" on page 15) and stitch six more rows around the lid. Change back to the main fabric and stitch five more rows around the lid.

3. Check the fit of the lid against the basket. When the edges of the lid touch the edges of the basket, take the lid to a surface with a grid such as a cutting mat. Pin the wrapped clothesline to the base of the lid to form a square around the base of the lid.

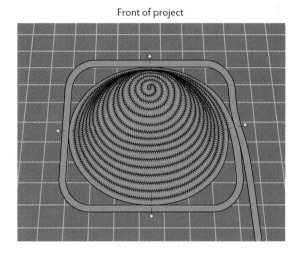

Front of project

4. Zigzag stitch the four sides of the square to the lid base at the center of each side. Zigzag stitch two more rows of clothesline around the square. There should be a gap in the lid at each of the corners. Fill the gaps with rows of wrapped clothesline cut to fit and stitch the clothesline in place. Fill any gaps by gluing squares of fabric into the small openings and stitching them in place.

5. Continue stitching rows of clothesline around the square base of the lid until the lid reaches the desired size. The lid should extend 1" beyond the side of the round base. Check the lid against your basket to be sure it fits and make any adjustments to the size as necessary. Once you have finished the lid, remove it from the machine, leaving the extra clothesline attached.

6. Taper off the clothesline to finish the lid.

7. Make and attach a handle to the lid (see "Ring-Style Handles" on page 58). Binding is optional.

KEEPING BASKET LIDS SECURE

There are three methods I like to use to help hold lids on baskets. The first method is to stitch medium-sized beads to the underside of the lid so the beads catch on the inside top edge of the basket, preventing the lid from moving around. The second method is to whipstitch a row of wrapped clothesline to the inside of the lid, creating a lip, so that the lip will catch on the inside top edge of the basket and prevent the lid from slipping off. This is a good method to use on flat lids. The third method is to shape the lid downward at the lower edge. This is done by changing to angle position 4 for the last three to five rows of the lid.

Method 1: Add Beads to the Inside of the Lid

1. To mark the placement of the beads, place the lid on the basket, aligning the fronts, and then turn the pair upside down. Push five or more straight pins into the lid around the outer edge of the basket, being sure to place a pin at the center front. Remove the basket and set the lid, with the pins intact, aside.

2. Stitch a medium-sized round bead about ⅜" to the inside of each pin. Check the fit of the lid on the basket after stitching on each bead.

Method 2: Add a Lip to the Inside of the Lid

1. To get the correct position for the lip, place the lid on the basket, aligning the fronts, and then turn the pair upside down. Push T-pins into the lid, around the outer edge of the basket. Remove the basket and set the lid, with the pins intact, aside.

2. Measure around the circumference of the lid at the pin marks using a tape measure, and then make a wrapped and zigzag-stitched length of clothesline a few inches longer than the measured circumference. Pin the outermost side of the clothesline ⅜" to the inside of the pins. Whipstitch the wrapped clothesline in place, removing the pins as you come to them. Check the fit of the lid on the basket often as you sew. When the lip is nearly finished and you have the correct fit, trim any excess clothesline. Hide the join with a small piece of fabric that is glued and stitched in place.

Method 3: Make the Lid Turn Downward at the Outer Edge

Change to angle position 4 (see page 18) when the lid is about ¾" smaller than the basket opening all around. Stitch in angle position 4 for 1", and then change to angle position 2 and add about four more rows. This makes the outer edge of the lid turn downward and helps keep the lid from sliding off the basket.

MORE LID IDEAS

CONE-SHAPED LID WITH TURNED-DOWN LOWER EDGE (FOR A ROUND BASKET)

This lid fits a basket that measures 7" in diameter. Make a round base coil consisting of two rows of clothesline, allowing a ¼" hole at the center. Add one row in angle position 1 and one row in angle position 2. Change to variation 1 of angle position 3 until the lid measures 3" high. Change to angle position 4 for 1" and then add 1 row of a contrasting fabric. Change to a coordinating fabric and add four more rows in angle position 2. Add a knotted handle accented with a large bead (page 59). The finished lid measures 4¼" high without the handle.

ROUNDED LID WITH A FLAT EDGE (FOR A ROUND BASKET)

From the collection of Jenny and Steve Rochon.

This lid fits a basket that measures 5¾" in diameter across the top. Make a round base coil that's 1¼" in diameter with a ¼" to ½" opening at the center. Add one row in angle position 1 and one row in angle position 2. Change to angle position 3 and continue until the lid measures 3½" from the center to the outer edge. Change to angle position 2 and continue until the lid measures 7¼" in diameter and hangs ¾" beyond the edge of the basket. Add a ring-style handle (page 58).

CONE-SHAPED LID
(FOR A ROUND BASKET)

This lid fits a basket that measures 8" in diameter across the top. Make a round base coil, consisting of two rows of clothesline, allowing a ½" opening at the center to accommodate a bulkier top embellishment. Add one row in angle position 1 and one row in angle position 2. Change to variation 1 of angle position 3 until the lid measures 5" from the center to the outer edge. Change to angle position 4 for 1" so the edge turns under slightly. The lid hangs over the basket by ¾". Bind the edge with a double binding. Add a handle (see "Handles with Coiled Bases" on page 60) and bead embellishments (page 65). The finished lid measures 6" high including the handle.

TIERED LID
(FOR AN OVAL BASKET)

This lid fits a basket that has a top opening of 9¼" x 7¼". To make the lid, make a 1"-wide oval base coil, starting with a 4" baseline and leaving a ¼" opening at the center. Add one row in angle position 1 and one row in angle position 2. Change to angle position 3 and continue until the lid measures 1¼" from the center to the outer edge. Change to angle position 4 and continue until the lid is about the same size as the basket. Change to position 2 and continue for 1". The lid should hang ¾" over the edge of the basket. Add a handle of knotted clothesline intertwined with gold cording and accented with beads (see "Knotted Handles" on page 59). A gold piece of jewelry adds a focal point. The finished lid measures 2½" high without the handle.

Handles

I frequently add handles to the sides of my baskets, and sometimes a handle that arcs across the top. For baskets with lids, I omit the handles from the basket and use one on top of the lid instead. This section offers several options for creating basket and lid handles. Choose a handle style and match it up with the basket or lid of your choice. Purse handles are discussed on page 40.

Flat clothesline handles accent the sides of this striped basket. For handle instructions, see page 56.

BASKET HANDLES

It is important to consider options for handles when you start a project; you may want to plan any fabric changes at the point of handle placement so the changes won't be as noticeable. A basket can be made with one handle that arcs over the top of a basket connecting the two sides, or with side handles positioned vertically or horizontally.

Keep the following guidelines in mind when creating handles:

- Handles need to be sturdy enough so the basket won't bend or become floppy when lifted.

- Hide the handle ends by tucking them underneath another portion of the project or by putting some embellishment over the end points.

- If making matching side handles, be sure to measure carefully and style the handles so they match. The second handle should be a mirror image of the first.

- When attaching handles with hand stitching, use needle-nose pliers to help pull the needle through the layers. Avoid using needles with large eyes because they will leave holes in the fabric.

Wrapped Clothesline Handles

I've found that the easiest handles are made from the same clothesline that you have been working with all along. Whether it is a single piece of clothesline or two or three sewn together side by side, the handles will be strong and easy to attach.

To make a handle from a single length of clothesline, simply wrap fabric strips around the clothesline in the same manner as for the basket. Use a little more glue on the back side of the fabric strips during the wrapping process to reduce fraying. Zigzag stitch along both edges or down the center of the clothesline to make a handle strip. If you are doing both edges, reduce the width of the zigzag stitch slightly from what was used on the basket so that the entire strip isn't covered with stitching. Form the strip into a loop or other shape and machine or hand stitch it securely to the basket, concealing the ends.

To make a knotted-loop side handle (above and detail below), tie a knot in the center of the clothesline, crisscross the ends, and secure them to the side of the basket. Buttons conceal the ends of the clothesline.

A triple-loop-and-tassel side handle was created using Whitney Design brand clothesline. This clothesline frays easily at the ends, making it perfect for creating a small tassel. Form the handle loops and hand stitch them firmly in place. Remove the fabric wrapping from the ends of the clothesline and fray the ends of the clothesline to make a tassel. Trim the tassel to the desired length and wrap thread around the top of the tassel to secure. Attach an accent bead just above the frayed ends of the clothesline.

A small round base coil was used for each side handle on this basket. Apply glue to the handle area that touches the basket and then stitch in place. A button accents the center of each coil.

A double-looped handle, resembling a heart, makes a nice side handle. A shank button conceals the ends of the clothesline.

For each of these side handles, an 18" length of wrapped clothesline was wrapped with contrasting thread and zigzag stitched just once down the center. The strip was loosely coiled and intertwined to make a web with openings. The resulting design was attached to the basket and embellished further with a cluster of beads.

To make this twisted handle (above and detail below), cut a thick piece of line (thicker than clothesline), wrap it with fabric strips, and secure with a glue stick. Shape the line by adding a twist in the middle and attach it to the basket, vertically, concealing the ends with beads. Wrap thread tightly around the handle, spacing rows of thread about $\frac{3}{8}$" apart and occasionally tacking in place.

For this side handle, extra-bulky clothesline was wrapped with a fabric strip and frayed at the ends. Look for clothesline that frays the same throughout. Clothesline that is too bulky for basket construction can be used for handles that don't require any machine stitching. This handle was additionally wrapped with textured cording and decorative thread, which was randomly hand tacked in place. To create the crescent shape of the handle, a wooden bead was stitched between the basket and handle, adding a nice arc to the center of the handle.

This single handle was created by braiding three rows of wrapped clothesline together and securing the ends to the sides of the basket. To help the handle retain its shape, hand tack the braided clothesline together in several places.

Flat Clothesline Handles

Flat handles can be created by stitching two or more lengths of bare clothesline together lengthwise, and then covering the resulting strip with fabric. These strips are easily manipulated into a variety of handle shapes. To make flat handle strips:

1. Zigzag stitch two or more lengths of bare clothesline together. Cut a piece of fabric large enough to wrap lengthwise around the strips, allowing enough for the raw edges to be folded under at least ¼". Press ¼" to the wrong side along one long edge of the strip.

2. Fold the fabric strip around the zigzag-stitched clothesline, positioning the folded edge of the fabric along one edge of the clothesline. Lightly glue in place, tucking the long raw fabric

edge to the inside. Topstitch along the long edges and down the center of the length as shown below.

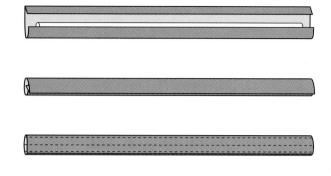

Two lengths of bare clothesline are zigzag stitched together, covered with a strip of fabric, and topstitched to make the handle strips (see "Flat Clothesline Handles," left). Join the ends of the strips at the top and wrap the join with a matching strip of fabric, turning in the raw edges. Stitch in place. Secure the top and bottom of the handle loop to the side of the basket as shown. Accent the handle and basket by attaching a large bead, wooden disks, and seed beads as shown.

Flat Webbing Handles

Nylon or polyester webbing makes a great handle on a basket and is often used on purses. A single layer or double layer can be used, depending how much support is needed. To use a double layer, simply layer two pieces of webbing; then glue and stitch them together along the sides. To match the handle to the basket, cover a 1"-wide strip of webbing with a 3"-wide strip of fabric. Fold and glue the fabric around the webbing in the same manner as for "Flat Clothesline Handles" (at left), pressing under ½" on one of the long side edges. Topstitch along both edges and down the center of the strip to complete the handle.

HALLOWEEN BASKET WITH FLAT WEBBING HANDLE

Nylon webbing is covered with a Halloween fabric to create a single handle that arcs between the sides of this basket. A coiled embellishment (below), accented with buttons, is stitched to each side of the handle to conceal the ends.

Twelve-inch strips of fabric-covered nylon webbing form the side handles on this basket. The handles extend to the bottom of the basket on the inside to conceal the starting and ending points for fabric changes. Buttons and beads were stitched on the outside of the basket over the center and ends of the handles.

LID HANDLES

Before constructing a lid for a project, always consider the handle design so you know how large an opening to leave for the handle at the top of the lid. I usually make my lid handles from wrapped clothesline. To attach the handle, I insert the ends into the opening in the lid, tie the ends in a knot, and then secure them to the underside of the lid with glue and hand stitching.

Flat Lid Handles

Flat lid handles are easily made by stitching two or more lengths of bare clothesline together lengthwise, and then covering the resulting strip with fabric. These flat strips work well for making horizontal handles that are perfect for oval basket lids. To make flat handle strips, see "Flat Clothesline Handles" (page 56).

Ring-Style Handles

An easy ring-style handle starts with one long piece of clothesline that is wrapped and zigzag stitched along the length. To make the handle, start with 44" of wrapped clothesline; thread a 3" piece of the wrapped clothesline down through the opening in the lid. Form a 1¾" loop on top of the lid with the remaining clothesline and thread the excess back to the inside of the lid. Come back up to the outside next to the starting point. Then wrap the clothesline through the loop over and over until you have either a loosely wrapped ring handle or a tightly wrapped ring handle with a ribbed effect. To finish, push the excess clothesline through to the inside and knot the ends. Trim off the excess clothesline. Glue and hand stitch the ends to the underside of the lid to secure.

A flat handle is centered over the top of this lid and attached at the two ends. To attach the handle, leave two holes in the oval base coil, one on each side of the lid, at the ends of the baseline. Bring the ends of the handle through the holes in the lid. Glue and hand stitch the handle ends to the underside of the lid.

A compact ribbed effect is achieved on this ring handle by wrapping the starting loop very tightly with additional wrapped clothesline.

Contrasting wrapped clothesline was used to make a circular knotted cluster for the top of this basket lid. A decorative bead was stitched to the center of the knotted cluster for added interest.

The ring handle on this basket has loose wraps around the ring for a loopy appearance.

Knotted Handles

Knots can produce an interesting handle with lots of texture. To make a knotted handle, tie knots in a length of wrapped clothesline until you achieve a pleasing design. Tying knots for a handle uses up a lot of wrapped clothesline. Always allow extra length. When finished making knots, attach the knotted cluster to the top of the lid, pulling the clothesline ends to the inside through the hole in the top of the lid. Strive to keep the handle looking balanced from all sides. Tie the ends in a knot on the underside of the lid. Trim off the excess clothesline; then glue and hand stitch the ends to the underside of the lid. For added interest, accent the knotted cluster with buttons, beads, decorative cording, or other embellishments.

An asymmetrical knotted handle accents this oval lid. Beads and decorative cord were intertwined with the knots in a pleasing arrangement. A piece of gold jewelry was attached to the front of the lid handle to create a focal point.

Looped Handles with Coiled Bases

A handle with a coiled base is made by first constructing the base, which is coiled exactly the same as the top of the lid it's attached to. Follow the directions for the lid, allowing the same size center opening, and finish off the base when it reaches about 1¼" high. Glue and tack the handle base to the top of the lid, aligning the center holes. For the looped handle, make a wrapped length of clothesline that is zigzag stitched down the center. Insert 3" of the covered clothesline to the inside of the lid and pin in place. Form five loops in the remaining length of clothesline and tack to the coiled base. Tightly wrap the remaining clothesline once around the bottom of the loops and tack in place. Insert the remaining clothesline to the inside of the lid. Tie the ends in a knot; then secure with glue and hand stitching. Trim off any excess clothesline.

To embellish this handle with a coiled base, wrap eyelash yarn around the loops and around the handle base in a random fashion and tack in place. Attach a gold button to the base of the handle and attach a couple of beaded dangles just under the button (see page 65 to make the beaded dangles).

Looped Handles

Looped handles add a dramatic look to a simple basket lid. Cut a 26" length of fabric that's 1½" wide. Fold the fabric in half lengthwise and press to make a ¾"-wide strip. Unfold the strip and fold the outer edges in to meet the fold on both sides. Press. Fold the strip in half and press again to make a ⅜"-wide strip. Stitch a narrow zigzag stitch down both edges. Fold the strip in half and make five loops in the strip, making the center loop slightly larger. Tack the loops together at the bottom. Push the ends of the looped handle strip through the hole in the lid center. Tie the ends together, trim off excess on the ends, glue, and tack in place.

The looped handle on this lid was made from the same fabric as the contrasting band, giving the project a coordinated appearance.

Embellishments

Embellishments range from subtle to dramatic. For a subtle effect, try using dimensional self-fabric flowers or other items that are similar in color to the project. For more impact, use embellishments that contrast with the project. Appliqué is a great way to add interest to a project and customize it for a holiday or special use. I often add beads and buttons to my projects, especially over handle ends to conceal the raw edges. I frequently bind the top edge of my projects. This conceals the end point of the clothesline used for constructing the basket, and when done in a contrasting fabric, it becomes a decorative border.

A pieced flower is appliquéd to the front of the basket (see "Appliqué" on page 62). Zigzag stitching helps protect the outer edges of the design.

APPLIQUÉ

Fused appliqué shapes work well on projects coiled from clothesline. Cut your own shapes or, for a very easy approach, cut a motif from printed fabric and fuse it to the project with fusible web. Use a mini-iron for hard-to-reach areas, like the inside bottom of a basket, and always follow the manufacturer's instructions for best results.

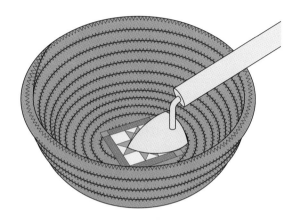

To protect the appliqué edges from fraying, use a machine zigzag stitch as shown on page 61 (if the project can be maneuvered under the presser foot), or add blanket stitching (see below).

BLANKET STITCHING

A blanket stitch is a decorative stitch that holds and protects the edges of a fused appliqué. Use two strands of embroidery floss or one strand of pearl cotton to make the decorative stitches. I sometimes use upholstery thread on my clothesline projects, as it doesn't tangle as easily as the others and it is strong enough not to ravel. Floss has six strands of thread, which can be separated to achieve the look desired. Pearl cotton is a thicker single strand that doesn't separate. Be sure to select a thread color that shows up against the fabric and keep your stitches uniform.

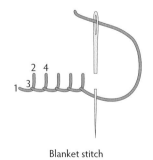

Blanket stitch

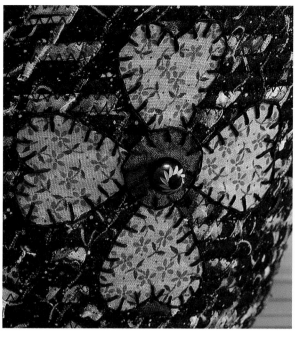

Two strands of black floss were used to blanket-stitch around this appliqué shape.

An appliquéd heart design is accented with blanket stitches.

DIMENSIONAL-FABRIC EMBELLISHMENTS

To create both spiral streamers and dimensional flowers with curled edges, I use a technique that was taught by Joan Shay on the television program *Simply Quilts*. To start, fuse two layers of fabric wrong sides together with HeatnBond UltraHold iron-on adhesive. Then cut out the desired motifs. For spiral streamers, cut long strips from layers of fused fabric and tightly wrap the strips around a bamboo stick or wooden dowel. Spread the streamers out along the stick so all the areas are heated evenly. Set the shape by pressing with an iron and allow it to cool. Then hand stitch the streamers to the project, being careful to maintain the shape. For flowers, cut out a flower shape and stitch it to the project in the desired position. Curl the edges around a bamboo stick or wooden dowel and press with a mini-iron.

A dimensional flower with spiraling streamers adds textural interest to an urn-shaped vessel. Use beads to accent the center of the flower. Tack the streamers to the basket, attaching a small bead at the stitching points.

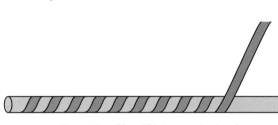

Wrap strips of fused fabric around a dowel and press to heat-set the shape.

Roll the edges of flowers over a wooden dowel and press to heat-set the shape.

Curled fabric flowers with bead centers give a simple round basket some dimensional interest. Layer flower shapes in graduating sizes to achieve this look. Add some short curled streamers around the edges of the flowers to resemble leaves.

DECORATIVE TRIMS AND THREADS

The projects in this book can be embellished with trims of all kinds. Use decorative cord or yarn to accent a lid handle or to add a separation line between the basket and binding at the top edge. Decorative threads can be used for blanket-stitching appliqués or to add texture to a beaded embellishment. One of my favorite threads is Ricky Tims's Razzle Dazzle Thread. It is designed for use in the bobbin, but I use it for hand stitching. The ends fray, so sometimes I incorporate that design element into my projects.

BUTTONS

Buttons of all shapes and sizes are available in stores—or in your mother's or grandmother's stash. Use two or more layers of buttons to add a focal point to a project, or use them to cover a handle's ending points. I often add colorful seed beads over the holes on the buttons.

Colorful buttons and seed beads add interest to this basket handle.

Ricky Tims's Razzle Dazzle Thread is used for attaching beads to this project. The frayed ends create a sparkling effect.

Layered buttons, accented with seed beads, become the focal point of this coiled embellishment.

Yarn and beads help to hide the transition between the top and bottom portions of this urn-shaped basket.

BEADS

I frequently use beads for embellishing projects. They can be used to help hide the ends of handles, to accent the centers of fabric flowers, or to dangle from a project. For added strength when beads are stitched directly to the project, after stitching apply a small amount of Fray Check to the threads that hold the beads in place.

To create dangles or tassels, thread several beads onto a long length of decorative multi-ply thread or cording and knot the thread under the beads to prevent them from falling off (make two knots if necessary). Leave excess length under the knot, and unravel and fray the bottom ends. Use the excess thread or cording at the top to attach the beaded dangle to your project.

Beaded dangle with frayed end

Beads are threaded onto satin cording tails. The cording tails are knotted together, then knotted separately, and then knotted together to create a diamond pattern at the end of the dangle. The ends are trimmed off next to the last knot and the cord is sealed with Fray Check.

Beaded dangles decorate the base of this lid handle. Select beads with holes large enough to slip onto the thread or cord. Beads with smaller holes can be tacked along the length of the cord separately, if desired.

A knotted cluster of beads embellishes the base of a basket handle. String a few beads at a time and tack them to the basket and handle randomly to create the clustered effect.

YO-YO FLOWERS

Yo-yos are easy embellishments to make and can be turned into flowers by simply adding a bead or button to the center. To make yo-yos, cut a circle that's about twice the diameter of the desired finished size. Turn ¼" to the wrong side of the circle and hand baste in place with running stitches. Pull the threads to gather up the circle. Knot the thread tails and trim the ends. Hand stitch the yo-yo to the project and stitch a bead or button to the center to make a flower.

For leaves, cut oval leaf shapes from Ultrasuede and hand or machine stitch to the project.

Yo-yo flowers are accented with beads, buttons, and Ultrasuede leaves.

WRAPPED-CLOTHESLINE EMBELLISHMENTS

Use wrapped clothesline to create interesting designs on the side of a project. Try wrapping thinner clothesline with fabric for a change in scale. Simply arrange the wrapped clothesline in the desired design, secure with a glue stick, and hand stitch in place.

Thin clothesline was wrapped and zigzag stitched as a single 12" unit, and then coiled to create these flowers. For dimension, straight stitch a Y shape so the flower can curl out. Add a bead or button at the flower center. Cut leaf shapes from fabric, zigzag the edges, and stitch them to the basket as desired.

Wrapped and zigzag-stitched clothesline in ⁹⁄₆₄" diameter was used to create a wavy design over the side of this breadbasket (see page 32). Glue, and then hand-tack the finished clothesline in place.

DOUBLE BINDING

Double binding reinforces the top or outer edge of a project and can be used to conceal the ending point of the clothesline. It can be done with contrasting fabric to create a border or with matching fabric for a subtle effect.

1. Cut a 2" strip across the width of the fabric and trim it to a length that is equal to the circumference of the edge you are binding plus about 6". Make a 45°-angle cut on one end.

2. Fold and press ¼" of the angled end to the wrong side. Fold the binding in half lengthwise and press.

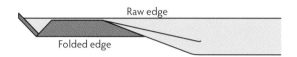

3. Align the raw edge of the binding with the upper outside edge of the project. Place the starting point where it will be least noticeable and pin. Starting 3" from the end, straight stitch ¼" from the long raw edges.

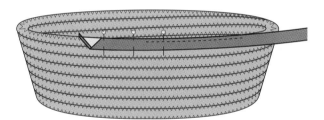

4. When you are almost back to the starting point, trim off the excess and insert the end of the binding into the fold at the beginning. Continue sewing the binding in place.

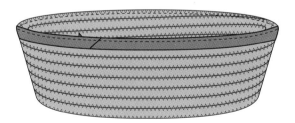

5. Turn the folded edge of the binding to the back or inside of the project, pin, and hand stitch in place.

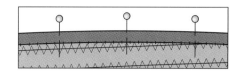

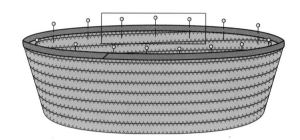

Coordinating double binding accents the edge of this flamingo plate.

Correcting a Bumpy Endpoint

If the ending spot of your clothesline is bumpy, insert a little batting or fabric into that spot before hand stitching the binding down. Another solution is to trim a small portion of the bump away and then sew your binding.

Gallery

Various fabrics were used to create a striped pattern on this vessel-shaped basket. To straighten the basket and bring the sides slightly inward near the top, use variation 2 of angle position 3 with the fingertip lift for the last several rows. The dramatic side handles are created from two pieces of bare clothesline stitched together and covered with matching fabric.

For this shoulder bag, I started with a wrapped and zigzagged oval base and partial side. A separate quilted center panel was made and attached to it. The upper edge of the quilted panel is accented with three additional rows of wrapped clothesline to tie it in with the base of the bag. Fabric-covered nylon-webbing straps complete the bag.

This clutch-style evening bag was designed with a custom-fitted zippered pocket on the inside to keep all essentials in the right place. A pointed flap with a Velcro closure is accented with a beaded tassel for an elegant look.

For Halloween I created this whimsical basket by using black, orange, and lime green fabrics along with some spider web appliqués and the letters *BOO!* cut from Ultrasuede. Blanket stitching , page 62, outlines the lettering. The handle is accented at the ends with a coiled design and buttons (see page 57).

A quaint cottage began as a square basket. After making a lid for the basket, I decided it didn't look properly proportioned, so I added another cone-shaped piece on top of the lid, securing it with glue and wrapping the join with another piece of wrapped clothesline. It became the perfect roof shape! To keep the roof on the cottage, I left a small slit in each corner of the lid during the construction. Then on the basket, I stitched a small coil in an upright position at each corner. The coils fit neatly into the lid slits, preventing the roof from coming off the cottage. To complete the cottage look, a door was blanket-stitched to the front of the basket and a window was added to the side. A window from contrasting fabric was attached to the door and side window and both were outlined with beads. A single bead was used as a doorknob. Beads also dangle from the peak of the roof.

The top and bottom portions of this urn-style basket are made as individual baskets first and then secured together with tacky glue and hand stitching. The last three rows of each of the baskets were made with contrasting fabric to produce the banded effect. The basket is embellished with beaded dangles and Ricky Tims's Razzle Dazzle Thread.

Decorator fabric was used to make this 8" whole-cloth plate. The plate was densely quilted with thread colors that matched each area of the plate. The heavy quilting draws the sides of the plate upward. A matching strip of fabric, with the inside raw edges turned under, was stitched around the outer edge of the plate. The outer threads were pulled to create the fringe.

This pastel baby basket (above), made from scrap fabrics, welcomed little Mia Weiss, daughter of Aaron and Suzanne Weiss, into the world. It can be used for storing small toys or baby essentials. Baskets make great baby gifts and all they take is your love and time!

This straight-sided round basket is made by alternating between two rows of contrasting fabric and two rows of a yellow fabric. All the rows start and end at the center front in order to be covered by the large front embellishment. Create the center design by coiling wrapped clothesline into an interesting design and accenting it with layered buttons and beads.

Create this V-shaped bowl by using variation 1 of angle position 3 for the sides. Embellish with a piece of copper wire wrapped around glass marbles and accented with bead dangles. To keep the embellishment components securely attached to each other and to the front of the bowl, I used an epoxy glue and hand stitching.

This basket and matching lid both feature center stripes. To keep the stripe centered on the basket when the lid is in place, stitch the stripe a little lower than center on the basket. Then when the lid hangs down slightly over the top portion of the basket, the stripe will be centered. A handle was designed from a length of beads.

The idea for this large basket came from an antique Oriental vase that I inherited from my parents. Large baskets can have stability problems, and this one became quite floppy. To solve the problem I stitched a brass ring inside the top edge of the basket and lined the interior edge with a layer of batting and fabric. The stair-step effect on the lid is achieved by repeating a sequence of angle positions several times. Wrapped clothesline creates textural interest over the surface of the lid.

A straight-sided basket is made with a striped pattern for a dramatic effect. Tab handles accented with buttons give this basket a unique look. A piece of clothesline is concealed in the top of each handle for stability.

An oval basket features a contrasting pieced band of color on the front, outlined with beads. A coordinating beaded embellishment was added to each side of the basket to complement the design. Simple loops of wrapped clothesline are used for the side handles.

Four fabrics were used to make this round striped basket. The flat clothesline handles on each side of the basket feature zigzag stitching on the edges in place of my usual three lines of straight stitching. The handles extend to the bottom of the basket on the inside to help conceal the starting and ending points for the fabric changes. A coil made from wrapped clothesline is attached to the outside of the basket over the end of each handle to conceal the raw edges.

A round basket with a flared upper edge is accented with coiled flowers. The flowers, created from wrapped clothesline, are accented at the centers with beads. Fabric leaves, finished with zigzag stitching, are tacked to the basket.